Schaf und Ruder / Wool and Water

# Schaf und Ruder / Wool and Water

Lili Dujourie, Isa Genzken,
Astrid Klein, Mischa Kuball,
Aron Mehzion, Reinhard Mucha,
Sturtevant, Rosemarie Trockel
& Gerhard Richter

Herausgegeben von / *Edited by*
Gregor Jansen
Kunsthalle Düsseldorf

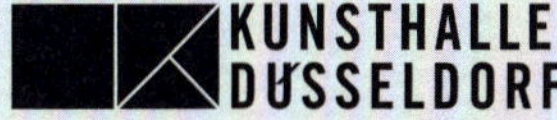


DISTANZ

# Seeing Everything, Understanding Nothing

Gregor Jansen

# Alles sehen, nichts begreifen

Gregor Jansen

**Preamble.** This exhibition and the accompanying catalog are very important to me, not just as a primarily aesthetic and emotional matter, but also a political one. The idea for this exhibition has occupied me for quite some time—since February 2012, to be precise—and it continued to develop with new thoughts, changes, and inspirations. Numerous conversations and discussions led me to various themes around the subject of mirrors and reflections, doublings and references. These continue to be the core of the exhibition, which essentially deals with a relationship to space—that is, looking and leading out from a sculptural perspective into the place where the exhibition occurs, into the museum and its history. On the one hand, it is about various questions in art itself, and on the other hand, about the reflection of our time and society, and not least the disintegrating human image today.

**Contemporary History.** In the analog age up to the last decade of the twentieth century, in theory and practice—for instance, in films such as *Playtime* (Jacques Tati, 1967) and *Blade Runner*[1] (Ridley Scott, 1982)—the way in which the reflection and doubling of the human being was understood as a model of knowledge had crucial effects: as a doubling in pictures, sculpture, or machines, based on descriptions of artificially created people and golems, of Kafkaesque doublings of absurd worlds. Jacques Lacan's paper "The Mirror Stage as Formative of the Function of the I" contains the foundation stone of countless attempts at interpretation and derivations of the question of self-consciousness. Gilles Deleuze in particular pointed to temporal divisions in *L'Image-mouvement: Cinéma 1* (1983) and *L'Image-temps: Cinéma 2* (1985) as a classification of images and symbols: the reflection opens our eyes to a new virtual space and results in a doubling of actual and imaginary perception. The mirror is thus a model for both: knowledge and illusion. Models were in vogue especially in the 1980s and 1990s as simplified images of reality (today people prefer to speak of theories or constructions). They were frequently used for aesthetic theories that dealt with the role of art in public and society, often in connection with studies by the sociologist Richard Sennett on the isolation, disorientation, and powerlessness of modern individuals in the urban environment (e.g. *The Fall of Public Man,* 1970). To this day, these questions remain as relevant as ever, and so mirrors as truth and deception can continue to function as starting points for central examinations and descriptions of the state of society.[2] One of the most impressive works of recent years is Jordan Wolfson's *Female Figure* (2014), a robot that interacts and speaks in front of a mirrored wall.

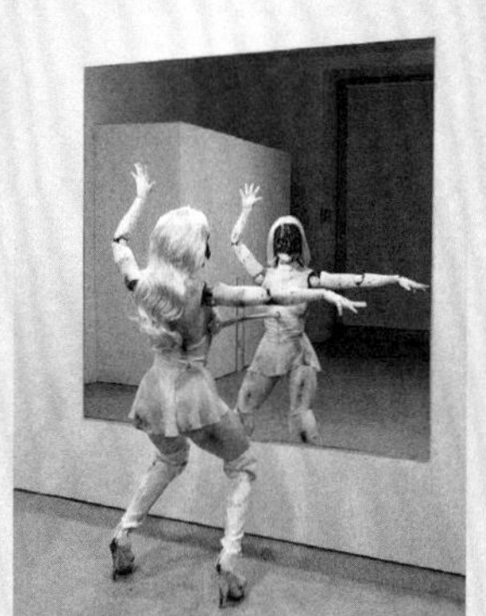

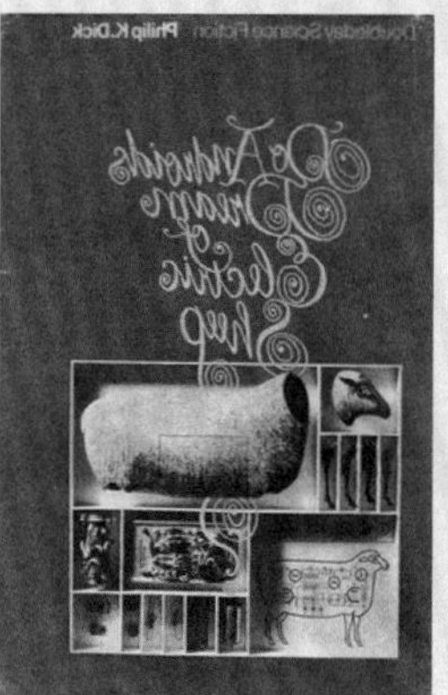

1

2

**Reflections.** "Seeing everything, understanding nothing." This is the explanation offered by Gerhard Richter for his *4 Panes of Glass* from 1967, these almost desperate demonstration objects by an objecting painter after the overburdened ism of the "capitalist realist"[3] who simply paints reproductions of banal photos. According to Richter, creating pictures reflects reality without commenting on it, and instead

**Präambel.** Diese Ausstellung und der sie begleitende Katalog sind mir sehr wichtig, nicht nur als vorrangig ästhetisches und emotionales Anliegen, sondern eben auch als politisches. Die Idee für diese Ausstellung beschäftigt mich seit geraumer Zeit, genau genommen seit Februar 2012, und immer wieder kam es zu neuen Überlegungen, Veränderungen, Anregungen. Zahlreiche Gespräche und Diskussionen führten in verschiedene Themenfelder rund um die Leitgedanken Spiegel und Spiegelungen, Verdopplungen und Referenzen. Sie bilden noch immer das Hauptanliegen, wobei es wesentlich um eine Beziehung zum Raum geht, also aus einer skulpturalen Perspektive heraus in den Ort des Geschehens, in die Kunsthalle und in ihre Geschichte schauend und führend. Einerseits geht es um verschiedene Fragestellungen in der Kunst selbst, andererseits aber auch um das Spiegelbild unserer Zeit und Gesellschaft, und nicht zuletzt um das brüchig gewordene Menschenbild heute.

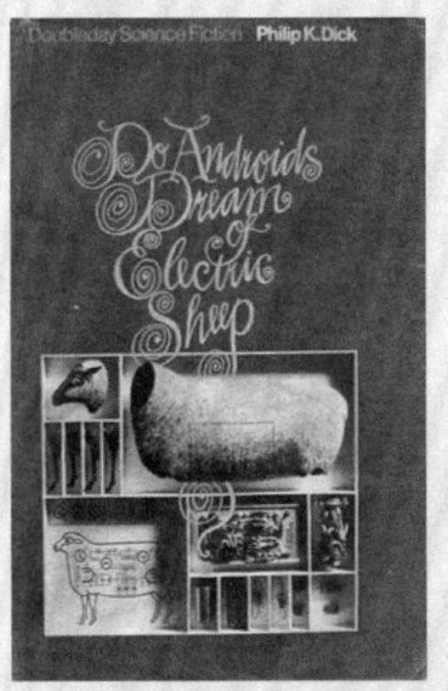


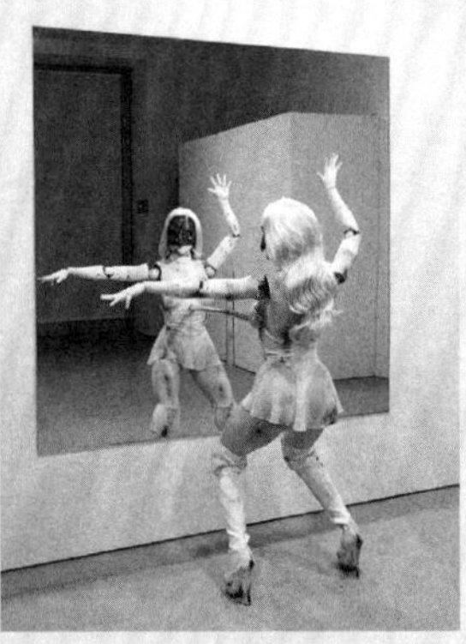

1 **Philip K. Dick,** Do Androids Dream of Electric Sheep?, Cover Erstausgabe Doubleday, 1968

2 **Jordan Wolfson,** Female Figure, 2014, Installationsansicht David Zwirner Gallery, New York, 2014

**Zeitgeschichte.** Im analogen Zeitalter bis zur letzten Dekade des 20. Jahrhunderts war es in Theorie und Praxis, beispielsweise in Filmen wie *Playtime* (Jacques Tati, 1967) oder *Blade Runner*[1] (Ridley Scott, 1982), von wesentlicher Wirkkraft, wie die Spiegelung und Dopplung des Menschen als Erkenntnismodell zu verstehen sei: als eine mediale Dopplung im Bild, der Skulptur oder Maschine, fußend auf Beschreibungen von künstlich geschaffenen Menschen und Golems, von kafkaesken Dopplungen absurder Lebenswelten. In Jacques Lacans Theorie *Das Spiegelstadium als Bildner der Ichfunktion* liegt der Grundstein unzähliger Deutungsversuche und Ableitungen in der Frage des Selbstbewusstseins. Vor allem Gilles Deleuze hat auf die Zeitspaltungen in *Das Bewegungs-Bild. Kino 1* (1989) und *Das Zeit-Bild. Kino 2* (1991) als eine Klassifikation von Bildern und Zeichen hingewiesen: Im Spiegelbild eröffnet sich unserem Blick ein neuer virtueller Raum, es kommt zu einer Verdopplung von aktueller und imaginärer Wahrnehmung. Der Spiegel ist somit ein Modell für beides: Erkenntnis und Täuschung. Modelle waren vor allem in den 1980er- und 1990er-Jahren en vogue als vereinfachtes Abbild der Wirklichkeit (heute spricht man lieber von Theorien oder Konstruktionen). Sie wurden für ästhetische Überlegungen, die sich der Rolle von Kunst in Öffentlichkeit und Gesellschaft zuwendeten, gerne herangezogen. Oftmals in Verbindung mit Untersuchungen des Soziologen Richard Sennett zu Vereinzelung, Orientierungslosigkeit und Ohnmacht moderner Individuen im urbanen Gefüge (z.B. *Verfall und Ende des öffentlichen Lebens. Die Tyrannei der Intimität,* 1983). Bis heute haben diese Fragestellungen nicht an Aktualität verloren, daher können Spiegel als Wahrheit und Täuschung weiterhin als Ausgangspunkte für zentrale Erkundungen und Zustandsbeschreibungen der Gesellschaft fungieren.[2] Eine der eindrucksvollsten Arbeiten der letzten Zeit ist *Female Figure* (2014) von Jordan Wolfson, ein vor einer Spiegelwand tanzender, interagierender und sprechender Roboter.

**Spiegelungen.** „Alles sehen, nichts begreifen", so erläuterte Gerhard Richter seine 1967 konstruierten *Gläser,* diese beinahe verzweifelten Demonstrationsobjekte eines sich verweigernden Malers nach dem arg überstrapazierten *Ismus* des „kapitalistischen Realisten",[3] der simpel gestrickt nur banale Fotos abmale. Das Herstellen von Bildern spiegele die Wirklichkeit kommentarlos wider, und statt Erkenntnis bringe es Tautologien hervor. Im Abmalen von Fotografien hatte Richter dafür 1962 die perfekte

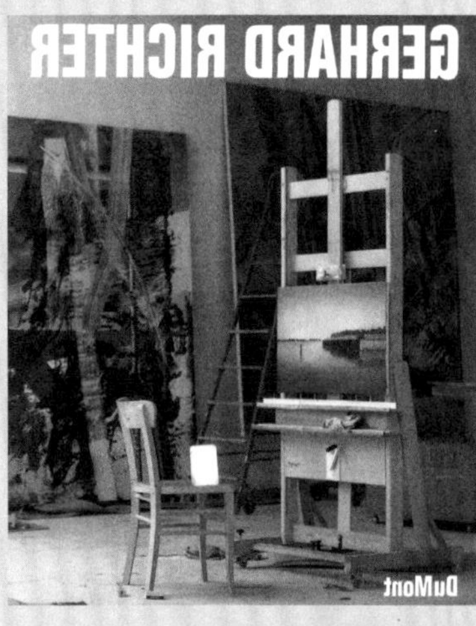


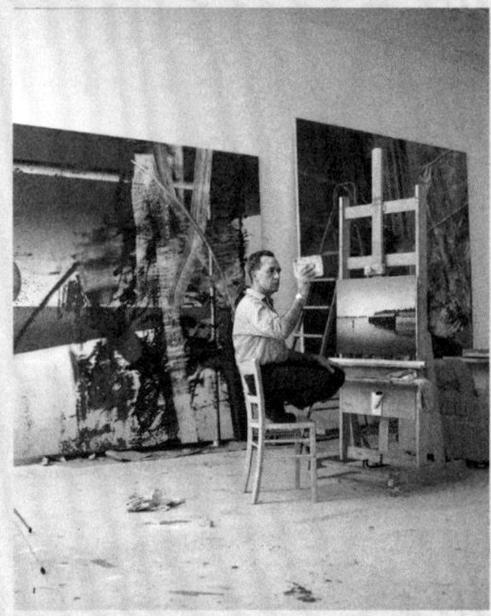

5

6

Fischer and knew Bim and Achim Reinert well, which is why he contributed one of his "girl" pictures to Creamcheese. For his 1981 exhibition at the Kunsthalle Düsseldorf, along with Georg Baselitz, Richter showed two identical mirrors in the Sidelight Hall, hung in close proximity to each other, as the catalog shows in a studio view from the back with a frontal view of Richter in the mirror.[5]

Then, in 1986, in his first major retrospective at the Kunsthalle Düsseldorf, Richter once again showed this legendary situation of two identical mirrors facing the building's only windows (figures 470-1 and 470-2 in the catalogue raisonné).[6] The conceptual work of the painter Richter is a clear, consistent model for perceiving visual reality. The mirror turns the gaze around; we see behind us, but if we really want to see what is behind us, we must turn around. An inverted world, just as the print of an image appears inverted. And it opens up a

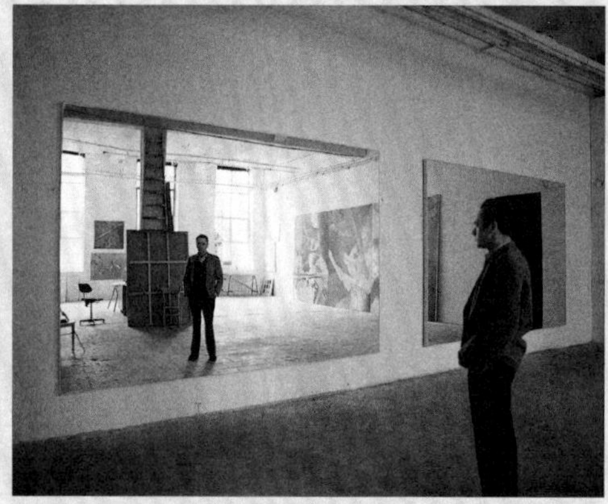

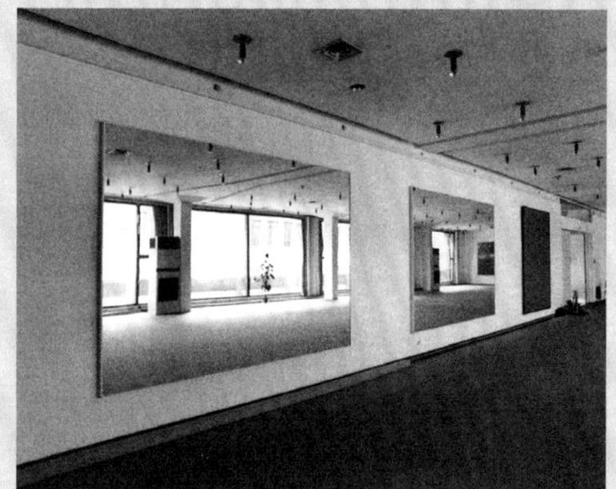

3

4

of insight it creates tautologies. By painting reproductions of photographs, in 1962 Richter found the perfect solution: he began with a designer table as a subject and overpainted it in an abstract, gestural style as a commentary on the zeitgeist. Surprisingly, this was followed in 1967 by these four panes of glass hung next to one another and rotatable around their transverse axis, like a Minimalist artwork, as clear and obvious as they were unsatisfying, since they only depict what they are: a view of the visible.[4] 1967 was also the year in which the Kunsthalle Düsseldorf opened, followed shortly thereafter by Konrad Fischer's gallery and Creamcheese, one of the first discos and artist's bars in Germany, not far from Grabbeplatz. Richter had a close friendship with

Ausführung gefunden, mit einem Designertisch als Motiv und dessen abstrakt-gestischer Übermalung als Zeitgeistkommentar ging es los. Überraschend folgten dann 1967 diese vier nebeneinander aufgehängten und über ihre Querachse drehbaren Glasscheiben. Wie ein Kunstwerk der Minimal Art, so klar und offenkundig wie unbefriedigend, stellen sie doch nur das dar, was sie sind: eine Sicht auf das Sichtbare.[4] 1967 ist aber auch d a s Jahr, in dem in Düsseldorf die Kunsthalle eröffnete, kurz darauf auch die Galerie von Konrad Fischer und das *Creamcheese* als eine der ersten Diskotheken oder Künstlerbars Deutschlands in unmittelbarer Nähe zum Grabbeplatz. Mit Fischer war er als Künstler eng befreundet, mit Bim und Achim Reinert gut bekannt, weswegen er für ihr *Creamcheese* ein „Mädchenbild" beisteuerte.

Bei seiner Ausstellung im Jahre 1981 in der Kunsthalle, gemeinsam mit Georg Baselitz, zeigte Richter zwei identische Spiegel im Seitenlichtsaal, eng nebeneinandergehängt, wie der Katalog es in einer Studioaufnahme mit der Rückenansicht vor und der Vorderansicht Richters im Spiegel wiedergibt.[5]

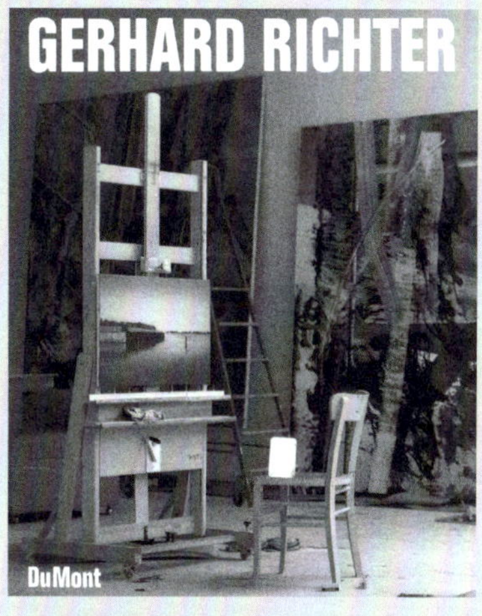


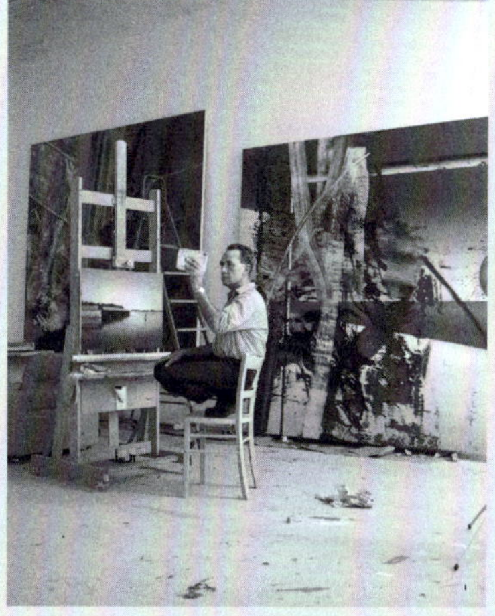

**5 Gerhard Richter,** Catalogue raisonné 1986, Cover

**6 Gerhard Richter** in seinem Studio, mit Spiegel in der Hand, 1985

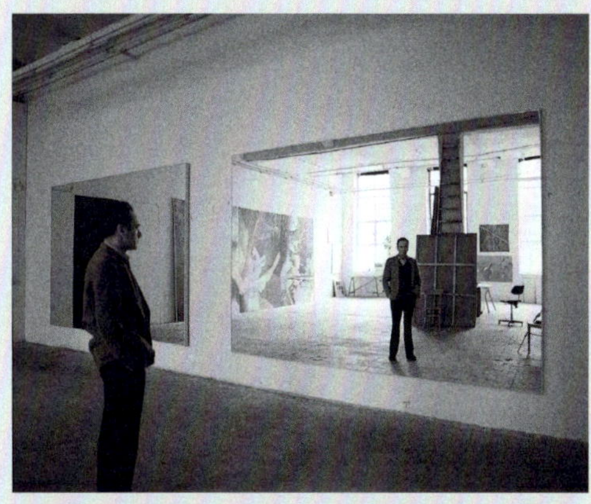

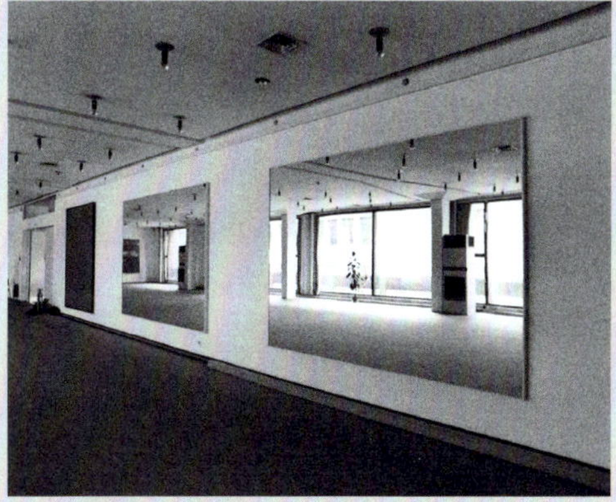

**3 Gerhard Richter,** zwei Spiegel im Studio, 1981, (WV-Nr. 470-1)

**4 Gerhard Richter,** zwei Spiegel in der Kunsthalle, 1981

Im Jahre 1986 zeigte Richter dann in der Kunsthalle Düsseldorf in seiner ersten großen Retrospektive diese legendäre Situation zweier gleicher Spiegel im Gegenüber der einzigen Fenster des Gebäudes erneut (Katalogabbildung im Werkverzeichnis mit den Nummern 470-1 und 470-2).[6] Das konzeptionelle Werk des Malers Richter ist ein klares, konsequentes Modell zur Erfassung der visuellen Wirklichkeit. Der Spiegel kehrt den Blick um, wir sehen hinter uns; wenn wir jedoch wirklich sehen wollen, was hinter uns liegt, müssen wir uns umdrehen. Seitenverkehrte Welt, wie der Abzug eines Bildes wiederum spiegelverkehrt erscheint. Und es eröffnet sich ein Raum nach hinten, hinter den Spiegel als eine virtuelle Dimension.

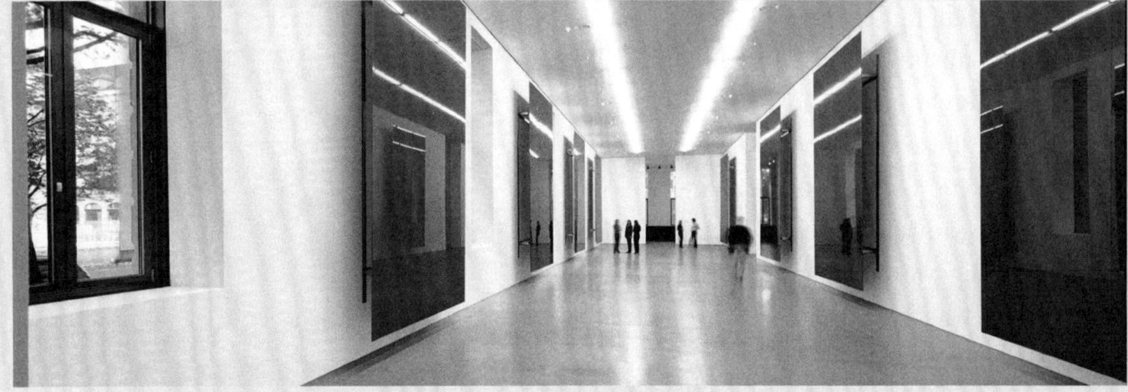

7

space that extends backward, behind the mirror as a virtual dimension.

While *Mirror* (1981, catalogue raisonné no. 470-2) is now at the Lenbachhaus in Munich, since 1981 its counterpart has belonged to the Kunsthalle Düsseldorf, an exhibition venue without a collection, or at least with only a very small and exclusive one. The cover of the catalogue raisonné compiled by Dietmar Elger shows Richter's studio with the small landscape painting *Venice (Island)* from 1985 on an easel. On the empty chair in front of the easel is a small mirror whose front does not reflect an image, but is pure white. Next to his biography in the appendix of the volume we see the same situation in a black-and-white photograph with Richter looking at his painting, examining, "checking" it as he gazes into the mirror, crouching with his feet on the seat of the chair.

Then, in 2002 his work *Eight Gray*, consisting of eight mirrors painted with enamel, was first shown at the Deutsche Guggenheim in Berlin.[7] Just as Richter's paintings create illusions—reflecting, reproducing, repeating—they simultaneously destroy them by emphasizing the part of the real world which comes to bear in painting. The gray reverse glass paintings reflect and direct the gaze backward, since there is no space beyond the neutral paint on the mirror. The paintings shatter reality with the chance photographic moment that they capture. The artist's narcissism is repelled by the recognition of the simultaneous truth and deception in the mirror. Richter disorients himself and us, and it is right that his oeuvre in retrospect does not result in a sum, a painterly or conceptual essence. But it is his enduring desire to produce images in any form which work independently and seemingly by themselves by constantly reflecting our gaze.

Then, however, ten years later, the key experience that preceded the aforementioned ideas, but only occurred in my work on the exhibition after the following event: During the exhibition tour marking Gerhard Richter's eightieth birthday in 2012 in London, Berlin, and Paris under the title *Panorama*, at the Neue Nationalgalerie in Berlin the work *Mirror* from the Kunsthalle Düsseldorf hung across from Richter's first painting, number 1 in the catalogue raisonné, *Table* (1962). I was delighted with this placement and the reverence shown to "our" *Mirror*, like a reflection of the first work, created precisely fifty years before, at the beginning of a glorious career, in Düsseldorf. Later I was fascinated to learn how this hanging came about: it refers to the first catalogue raisonné from 1986, in which Richter's very first work, *Table*, was shown in an inverted image—although to this day only very few people have noticed. I could not stop thinking about this constellation and the many parameters of an artwork that has a very

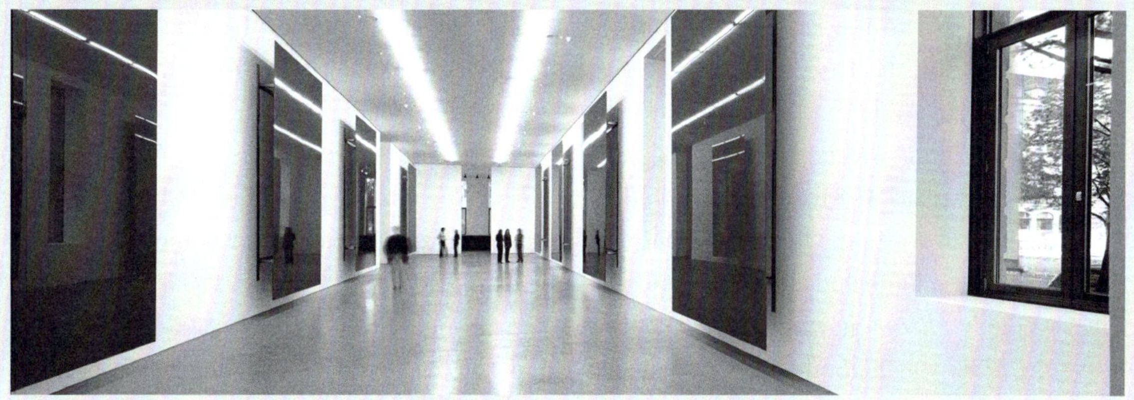

**7** **Gerhard Richter,** Acht Grau (Eight Grey), 2002, Ausstellungsansicht Deutsche Guggenheim, Berlin 2002

Während *Spiegel* (1981) mit der Werkverzeichnisnummer 470-2 sich heute im Lenbachhaus in München befindet, gehört das Pendant bekanntlich seit 1981 der Kunsthalle Düsseldorf, einem Ausstellungshaus ohne Sammlung oder mit zumindest einer sehr kleinen, exklusiven. Das Cover dieses von Dietmar Elger erstellten Catalogue raisonné zeigt die Ateliersituation von Richter, eine Staffelei mit dem aufgespannten kleinen Landschaftsbild *Venedig (Insel)* von 1985. Auf dem leeren Stuhl vor der Staffelei steht ein kleiner Spiegel, dessen Vorderseite aber kein Bild erscheinen lässt, sondern rein weiß ist. Neben seiner Biografie im Anhang des Katalogs, sieht man dieselbe Situation in einer Schwarz-Weiß-Abbildung, wo Richter mit den Füßen auf der Sitzfläche des Stuhls hockend mit dem Blick in den Spiegel seine Malerei anschaut, prüft, „kontrolliert".

2002 dann die Grauen Spiegel, acht an der Zahl, zuerst gezeigt in der Deutschen Guggenheim Berlin.[7] So wie Richters Gemälde Illusion erschaffen – spiegelnd, reproduzierend, wiederholend –, zerstören sie diese zugleich, indem sie den Anteil an Realem in den Vordergrund stellen, der in der Malerei wirksam ist. Die grauen Hinterglasbilder spiegeln und werfen den Blick zurück, denn es gibt keinen Raum jenseits der neutralen Spiegelfarbschicht. Die Gemälde lassen die Realität an dem zufälligen fotografischen Moment zerschellen, den diese festhalten. Der Narzissmus des Künstlers erschrickt vor der Erkenntnis der gleichzeitigen Wahrheit und Täuschung im Spiegel. Richter irritiert sich und uns, und es ist schon richtig, dass sein Œuvre im Rückblick keine Summe ergibt, eine malerische oder inhaltliche Essenz. Jedoch ist es ein stetes Begehren, Bilder jedweder Form hervorzubringen, die eigenständig und wie von selbst funktionieren, indem sie unseren Blick permanent zurückwerfen.

Dann aber, zehn Jahre später, das Schlüsselerlebnis, welches den beschriebenen Überlegungen zwar zeitlich voransteht, in meiner Arbeit zur Ausstellung aber erst nach folgendem Ereignis geschah: Zur Ausstellungstournee und Retrospektive anlässlich Gerhard Richters 80. Geburtstags im Jahre 2012 in London, Berlin und Paris unter dem Titel *Panorama* hing der *Spiegel* aus der Kunsthalle Düsseldorf in der Berliner Neuen Nationalgalerie gegenüber dem ersten Gemälde Richters, der Werkverzeichnisnummer 1, dem *Tisch* (1962). Ich war hocherfreut über diese Platzierung und die Referenz, die damit „unserem" *Spiegel* zuteil wurde, gleichsam als Spiegelung des ersten Werks, entstanden genau 50 Jahre zuvor, zu Beginn einer glanzvollen Karriere, in Düsseldorf. Spannend war es letztlich, als ich aufgeklärt wurde, warum es zu dieser Hängung gekommen war: Sie verweist auf eben jenen ersten Œuvrekatalog aus dem Jahre 1986 zurück, in dem der Fauxpas einer seitenverkehrten Abbildung genau des ersten Werks Richters, dem *Tisch,* geschah – was jedoch kaum und bis heute nur sehr wenigen Betrachtern aufgefallen ist. Mich ließ diese Konstellation bzw. die vielen Parameter eines Kunstwerks, welches eine sehr enge Beziehung zur Kunsthalle Düsseldorf besitzt – ich würde behaupten,

close relationship to the Kunsthalle Düsseldorf—comparable to Joseph Beuys's *Black Hole,* I would say—and they continue to fascinate me. *Black Hole* was created at the Kunsthalle Düsseldorf in 1981 for the exhibition *Schwarz,* with a stove pipe that extends to the outside of the building and ends at the facade. Like Richter's *Mirror,* it was also left to the museum. 1981 was a good year for the institution, then barely twenty-five years old. And in the same year Reinhard Mucha created his *MÄNNER FRAUEN* at the Kunstakademie—but more on that later.

**Through the Looking-Glass.** Here it already becomes clear why the exhibition *Schaf und Ruder / Wool and Water* is closely linked with the architecture and the institution of the Kunsthalle Düsseldorf itself. It represents a spatial experiment with various levels of depiction and asks questions about what art, artworks, work, the world, the self, and its reflections can be as models of knowledge. Behind the mirror, paradoxically a concrete frame of reference opens for our questions about the real and a reality that lies between things. Thus, the exhibition explores knowledge, values, and correlations both as a central question and answer in space. It aims to mark an intermediate space, a free space or place for freedom between two things. Which brings us to the title of the exhibition: *Schaf und Ruder / Wool and Water* is the fifth chapter in Lewis Carroll's 1871 novel *Through the Looking-Glass, and What Alice Found There.* This is the chapter in which Humpty Dumpty appears,[8] a character who is almost completely unknown in the German-speaking world. In the phonetic juxtaposition of a-a/u-u and in the reflection of the meanings of sheep-wool and oar-water lies a linguistic metaphor in one of the most fascinating books of literary history. The sequel to *Alice's Adventures in Wonderland* (1865) shows us the world behind the mirror and opens up countless levels of interpretation between the Victorian period and antiauthoritarian child-rearing. Carroll's story has also become an important part of pop culture, not least through the eccentric movie adaptations of the two books by Tim Burton in 2010 and 2016. Christian Enzensberger, who translated *Alice* into German in 1963, precisely described the dilemma they contain:

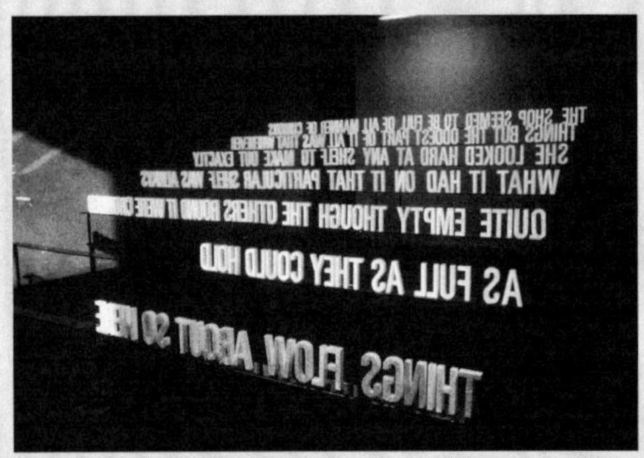

8

> Carroll's books deal with society . . . . In the lands that Alice wanders through, people die the deaths of embarrassment and having to remain silent; people aren't murdered here, but are silenced; and their throats aren't cut, but they are cut off from answering. Alice suddenly finds herself in a labyrinth, in a house of mirrors of proper behavior.[9]

Rüdiger Schöttle made a direct reference to the fifth chapter of *Through the Looking-Glass* in 1988 with his installation *Wool and Water.*[10] The chapter title *Wool and Water* is a metaphor for Great Britain's early industrialization and naval power. Originally conceived for a shop window at Victoria Miro Gallery on Cork Street in London, where it could only be viewed from outside, the work deals with the interaction between products and commerce, the presentation and perception of artistic work. It reflects our relationship to art, which has continually changed since the industrial revolution. The approximately twenty-centimeter-high

dieselbe, die auch *Das Schwarze Loch* von Joseph Beuys innehat, nicht mehr los und beschäftigten mich immer wieder. *Das Schwarze Loch* war im Jahre 1981 anlässlich der Ausstellung *Schwarz* innerhalb der Kunsthalle entstanden, mit einem Ofenrohr, das nach außen führt und an der Fassade endet. Es wurde ihr wie der *Spiegel* von Richter ebenfalls überlassen. 1981 war ein gutes Jahr für die damals knapp 25 Jahre alte Institution. Und in eben jenem Jahr fertigte Reinhard Mucha in den Werkstätten der Kunstakademie am Eiskellerberg sein *MÄNNER FRAUEN*, doch dazu später.

**Through the Looking-Glass.** Deutlich wird bereits hier, warum die Ausstellung *Schaf und Ruder / Wool and Water* eng mit der Architektur und der Institution der Kunsthalle selbst verknüpft ist. Sie bildet eine räumliche Versuchsanordnung vielschichtiger Darstellungsebenen und möchte Fragen danach stellen, was Kunst, Werk, Arbeit, Welt, das Ich und dessen Widerspiegelung als Erkenntnismodelle sein können. Hinter dem Spiegel eröffnet sich paradoxerweise ein konkreter Referenzrahmen für unsere Fragen an das Reale und an eine Realität, die zwischen den Dingen liegt. Das Ausloten von Erkenntnis, Werten und Korrelationen steht in der Ausstellung somit zentral parallel als Frage und Antwort im Raum. Es geht um das Ausmachen eines Zwischenraums, einen freien Raum oder einen Ort der Freiheit zwischen zwei Dingen. Womit wir beim Titel der Ausstellung wären: „Schaf und Ruder" bzw. „Wool and Water" lautet das fünfte Kapitel in Lewis Carrolls Erzählung *Alice hinter den Spiegeln (Through the Looking-Glass, and What Alice Found There)* aus dem Jahre 1871. In diesem Kapitel taucht Humpty Dumpty auf, die Figur eines sprechenden Eies,[8] die in der englischsprachigen Welt berühmt, im deutschsprachigen Raum jedoch so gut wie unbekannt ist. Im phonetischen Gegenüber von a-a/u-u und in der Spiegelung der Bedeutung von Schaf/Wolle und Ruder/Wasser liegt ein sprachlicher Bildbezug in einem der faszinierendsten Bücher der Literaturgeschichte. Die Fortsetzung von *Alice im Wunderland* (*Alice's Adventures in Wonderland*, 1865) lässt uns direkt hinter den Spiegel schauen und eröffnet unzählige Interpretationsebenen zwischen Viktorianischem Zeitalter und antiautoritärer Erziehung. Carrolls Erzählung ist außerdem ein wichtiger Bestandteil der Popkultur geworden, nicht zuletzt durch die wahnwitzige Fantasyverfilmung beider Bücher von Tim Burton in den Jahren 2010 und 2016. Christian Enzensberger übersetzte die *Alice*-Bücher 1963 ins Deutsche und beschrieb das ihnen inhärente Dilemma wie folgt:

> Carrolls Bücher handeln von der Gesellschaft […] In den Ländern, die Alice durchwandert, stirbt man die Tode der Verlegenheit und des Verstummenmüssens; man wird nicht ermordet, sondern mundtot gemacht; und nicht die Gurgel wird einem abgeschnitten, wohl aber die Antwort. Unversehens ist Alice in einen Irrgarten, in ein Vexierspiegelkabinett des schicklichen Verhaltens geraten.[9]

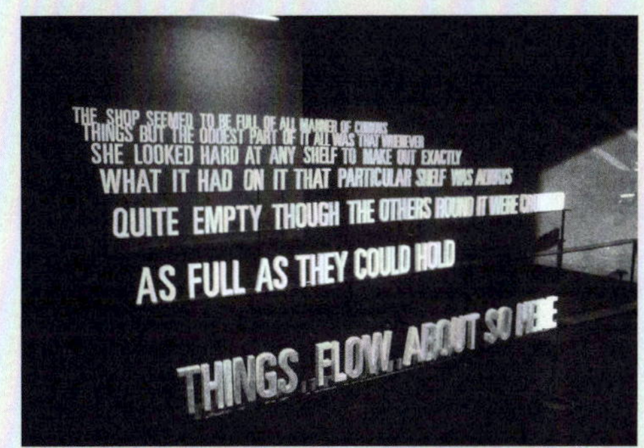


8 **Rüdiger Schöttle,** Wool and Water, 1988
Installationsansicht: Victoria Miro Gallery, London, 1988

Eine direkte Bezugnahme auf das fünfte Kapitel von *Alice hinter den Spiegeln* schuf im Jahre 1988 Rüdiger Schöttle mit seiner Installation *Wool and Water.*[10] Die Kapitelüberschrift *Wool and Water* ist eine Metapher für Großbritanniens frühe Industrialisierung und die Flotte des Königreichs. Ursprünglich für ein Schaufenster der Galerie Victoria Miro in der Londoner Cork Street konzipiert und nicht begeh-, da nur von außen einsehbar, thematisiert die Installation die Wechselbeziehung zwischen Warenwelt und Kommerz, Präsentation und Perzeption künstlerischer Arbeit. Sie reflektiert unsere seit der Industrialisierung sich stets verändernde Beziehung

styrofoam letters are coated in white pigment that glows blue under a black light and at the time revealed its full effect in the dark winter months. This made the quotation seem to float in space and created a distressing experience that challenged visitors to question their expectations and belief in what is real.[11]

The installation is structured like a grandstand and sits on stacked panes of glass that extend across the exhibition space. They allude to the following sentence from Carroll's novel:

> The shop seemed to be full of all manners of curious things but the oddest part of it all was that whenever she looked hard at any shelf to make out exactly what it had on it that particular shelf was always quite empty though the others round it were as full as they could hold.

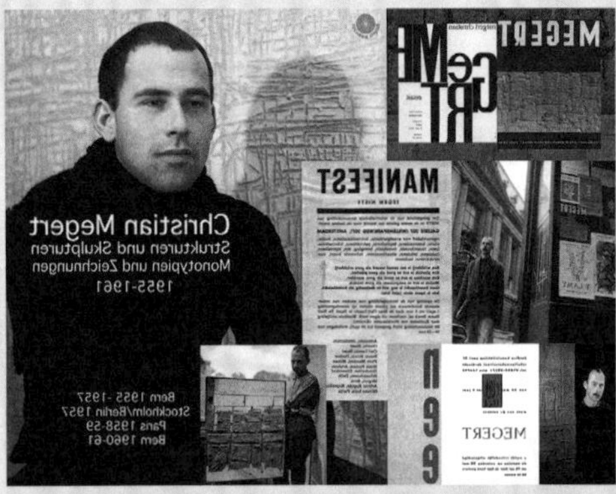


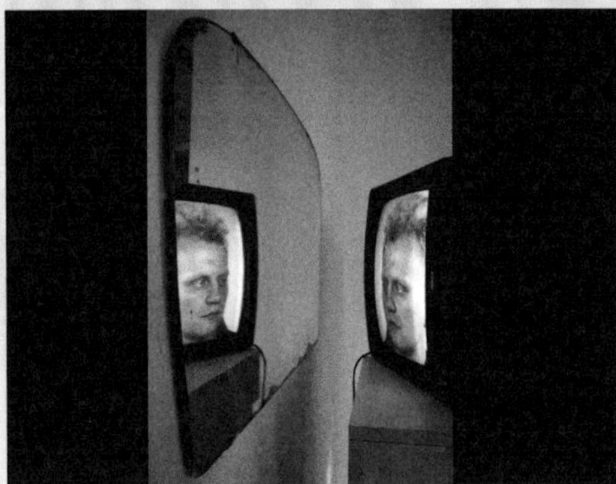

9

10

**Narcissus.** Human beings have long been fascinated by mirror images and their doubling as well as the reflection of the invisible in the myth of Narcissus, who fell in love with his own reflection in a pool. The origin of the myth is disputed: ancient Greek and Roman sources describe Narcissus as a beautiful young man, while an earlier source from Eritrea portrays him as a powerful god of nature. Yet the real space between the viewer, the water as a life-giving, reflective element, and the fictional, imagined speculative space behind this surface is no doubt significant. To this day, this has resulted in numerous psychological and philosophical conjectures centered around the human image or the effects of narcissism on society, even including mass phenomena and psychograms of our "narcissistic society."[12] Many artists, such as Robert Smithson, Robert Morris, and Dan Graham, began using mirrors in the 1960s and formulated a penetratingly real and speculative (as in the Latin word speculum for "mirror," now used to refer to a medical instrument) view of—and especially behind—the essence of things, and another perspective on the possibility of knowledge and its representability.[13] In 1961 Christian Megert wrote his manifesto "Ein neuer Raum" on the occasion of his exhibition at Arthur "Addi" Køpcke's gallery in Copenhagen. The manifesto was a call to "use art to rethink all things spatial."[14] Space and its conditions have been subjected to sociopolitical examination, and ideas such as transparency, reflection, and projection have applied the social-critical vocabulary of time to art. The individual and the concept of the subject have also undergone a liberation and a new questioning.

A more recent example of a Narcissist complex was created by the Düsseldorf artist Ralf Berger in 1998 with his video *Self-Begotten (True Love).* In it, the artist stands close to an old mirror. The mirror can be recognized in the later video due to the traces of wear on it. The artist gazes incessantly into his own eyes. In an intricate creation story, the text that

zur Kunst. Die etwa 20 Zentimeter hohen Styroporbuchstaben sind mit weißem Pigment beschichtet, das bei Schwarzlicht blau aufleuchtet und damals seine volle Wirkung in der dunklen Winterzeit entfaltete. Dadurch schien das Zitat im Raum zu schweben und erzeugte ein verstörendes Erlebnis, das den Betrachter aufforderte, seine Erwartungen und den Glauben an das, was „real“ war, zu hinterfragen.[11]

Die Installation baut sich ähnlich einer Tribüne auf und steht auf gestaffelten Glasplatten, die sich über den Ausstellungsraum erstrecken. Sie zitieren folgenden Satz aus dem Roman von Carroll:

> The shop seemed to be full of all manners of curious things but the oddest part of it all was that whenever she looked hard at any shelf to make out exactly what it had on it that particular shelf was always quite empty though the others round it were as full as they could hold.

**Narziss.** Seit Menschengedenken fasziniert sowohl das Spiegelbild und seine Verdopplung als auch die Reflexion des Nichtsichtbaren im Mythos von Narziss, der sich in sein eigenes Spiegelbild im Wasser verliebt. Nicht einig ist man sich in Bezug auf den Ursprung des Mythos, da hellenistisch-römische Quellen Narziss als jungen Schönling schildern, hingegen eine frühere Quelle aus Eritrea Narziss als mächtige Naturgottheit darstellt. Bedeutsam jedoch ist zweifellos der reale Raum zwischen dem Betrachter, dem Wasser als Lebens- und Spiegelelement und dem fiktiven, imaginierten spekulativen Raum hinter dieser Oberfläche. Daraus entstanden bis heute zahlreiche psychologische und philosophische Überlegungen, in deren Zentrum das Menschenbild bzw. die Auswirkungen des Narzissmus auf die Gesellschaft stehen, bis hin zum Massenphänomen und Psychogramm unserer „narzisstischen Gesellschaft“.[12] Zahlreiche Künstler wie Robert Smithson, Robert Morris oder Dan Graham verwendeten ab den 1960er-Jahren Spiegel und formulierten eine eindringlich reale wie spekulative (lat. speculum: Spiegel, oder medizinisches Untersuchungsgerät) Tiefensicht auf und dann vor allem hinter das Wesen der Dinge – eine andere Sicht auf die Möglichkeit von Erkenntnis und ihrer Darstellbarkeit.[13] Christian Megert verfasste 1961 gar das Manifest *EIN NEUER RAUM* anlässlich seiner Ausstellung bei „Addi“ Køpcke in Kopenhagen. Das Manifest war ein Aufruf, mit der „Hilfe von Kunst alles Räumliche neu zu überdenken“.[14] Der Raum und seine Bedingungen wurden soziopolitisch untersucht und Begriffe wie „Transparenz“, „Reflexion“ und „Projektion“ übertrugen das gesellschaftskritische Vokabular der Zeit in die Kunst. Ebenso standen das Individuum und der Subjektbegriff vor einer Befreiung und Neubefragung.

Ein jüngeres radikales Beispiel eines narzisstischen Komplexes schuf der Düsseldorfer Ralf Berger 1998 mit seinem Video *Self-Begotten (True Love).* Der Künstler steht darin nah vor einem alten Spiegel. Dieser ist aufgrund seiner Gebrauchsspuren

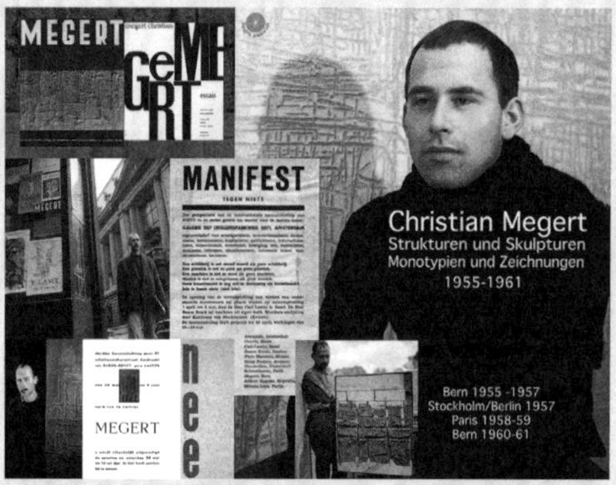


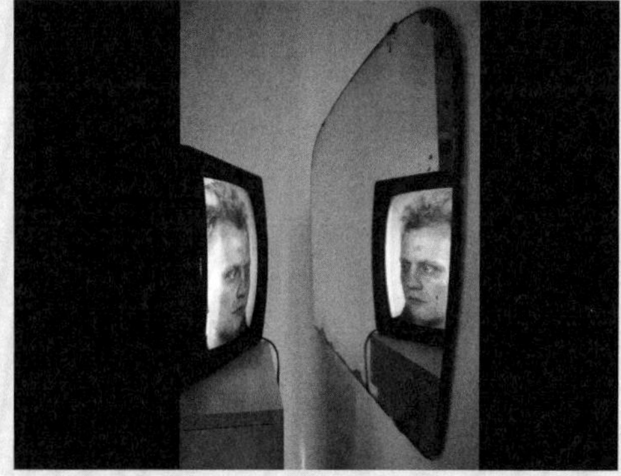

**9 Cover Christian Megert:** Strukturen und Skulpturen, Monotypien und Zeichnungen, 1955–1961, 2002, Film von Franziska Megert (Konzeption, digitale Ausführung)

**10 Ralf Berger,** Self-Begotten (True Love), 1998

auf dem späteren Video wiedererkennbar. Der Künstler sieht sich ununterbrochen in die Augen. Der Text, der das Video begleitet, gibt in einer ver-

accompanies the video makes reference to the meaning of "self-begotten" and to the fact that all kinds of monstrous fabulous creatures can be created in the process of self-begetting, one of which might be the artist himself. The video was later reflected: it shows the actual reflection of the original performance in front of the original mirror installed on the wall. The text is also reflected and can only be read in the mirror. The viewer is given no indication that the artist, while he looks intensely into his own eyes, is masturbating.[15] The artist himself can no longer say when the "self-begetting" took place, since afterward he remained standing in front of the mirror for an indefinite period of time. Any form of physical "love" could ultimately only be self-satisfaction with or from another body.[16]

**Analog versus digital—and this brings us to the exhibition itself.** Doubling, reflecting, and cloning lead to absurd scenarios. The digital monitoring of the micro and macro worlds is changing the organic composition of human perception. Pictures of people, mummified surfaces of phenomena, contrast strikingly with images without a visible background. Nonetheless, the sensory and intellectual double reference to the world must remain intact, and perception must include an individual and collective cultural memory. A gigantic multiverse of images spans between codes and physiology, between circuits and plotters. Do people today know how they look, what they would dare to dream on the other side of the mirror, and above all, how they are feeling? The reflection has become fragmented, broken, and the dream that it embodies has nearly collapsed. The exhibition *Schaf und Ruder / Wool and Water* brings together artists in regard to various aspects of their relationship to space and images, the perspective of "multiversal" reflections, doublings, or references. The important part is the sculptural relationship to space and not so much the pure pictorial surface as a reflection of the real as a revelation of the imaginary without the symbolic.

**Men versus Women.** Following from this, beginning with space and the genre of sculpture, two central questions emerge regarding our positioning in space and the picture as an imaginary foil of real objects. Since 2012, various parameters and constellations have been considered in the conception of the exhibition. It was by no means meant to be an iconographic exhibition that would focus on variations of the use of mirrors starting from a certain point in time. Rather, it was meant to revolve around the role of the Kunsthalle Düsseldorf in experimenting with and exploring contemporary problems, based on a history and identity of the institution and the context. Richter and his *Mirror* in a non-collection as well as the doubling and referentiality on multiple levels would provide the essential references: Düsseldorf and Cologne, the specific situation of the Kunsthalle Düsseldorf since 1966 (the current building was opened in 1967) and the year 1981, and the interactions between the Rhineland and Belgium (with Marcel Broodthaers as an example). In the beginning, the exhibition was conceived along the lines of this axial symmetry, and what ultimately remained was the most important exponent since 1967, the opening year of the Kunsthalle Düsseldorf: Lili Dujourie. All the aspects that reflect the framework of *Schaf und Ruder / Wool and Water* come to bear in her oeuvre, just as they do in Mucha's.[17]

**Lili Dujourie's** works, since her first piece from 1967, have conveyed an understanding of problems between form, content, and space, between strict conception and sensual materiality, balance and gravity. Her reinterpretations of themes, forms, and gestures from art

klausulierten Schöpfungsgeschichte Hinweise auf die Bedeutung des Self-Begotten und darauf, dass in dem Prozess des Selbsterschaffens allerlei monströse Fabelwesen entstehen können, von denen der Künstler möglicherweise selbst eines darstellt. Das Video ist im Nachhinein gespiegelt worden: Es gibt vor dem an der Wand installierten Originalspiegel das tatsächliche Spiegelbild der Originalperformance wieder. Auch der Text ist gespiegelt und kann nur im Spiegel gelesen werden. Der Betrachter erhält keine Information, dass der Künstler, während er sich intensiv und gegenstandslos in die eigenen Augen sieht, masturbiert.[15] Der Künstler kann selbst nicht mehr sagen, wann es zur „Selbsterschaffung" gekommen war, denn danach ist er noch für unbestimmte Zeit vor dem Spiegel stehen geblieben. Jegliche Form der körperlichen „Liebe" könnte letzten Endes auch nur eine Selbstbefriedigung mit oder an einem anderen Körper darstellen.[16]

**Analog versus digital – und damit zur Ausstellung selbst.** Die Dopplung, das Spiegeln oder das Klonen verhelfen zu absurden Szenarien. Die digitalisierte Monitorisierung der Mikro- und Makrowelt verändert die organische Zusammensetzung menschlicher Wahrnehmung. Bilder vom Menschen, mumifizierte Oberflächen der Phänomene, stehen in auffallender Rivalität zu Bildern ohne sinnlich erkennbaren Hintergrund. Dennoch muss der sinnlich-geistige Doppelbezug zur Welt erhalten bleiben, muss die Wahrnehmung ein individuelles wie kollektives kulturelles Gedächtnis umspannen. Ein gigantisches „Bildermultiversum" spannt sich zwischen Codes und Physiologie, zwischen Schaltungszuständen und Plottern auf. Weiß der heutige Mensch noch, wie er aussieht, was er sich hinter den Spiegeln zu erträumen wagte, und vor allem, wie es um ihn steht? Sein Spiegelbild ist brüchig geworden, zerbrochen, und der ihm innewohnende Traum nahezu geplatzt. Die Ausstellung *Schaf und Ruder / Wool and Water* vereint Künstlerinnen und Künstler unter verschiedenen Aspekten der Raum- und Bildbeziehung, der Perspektive „multiversaler" Spiegelungen, Dopplungen oder Reflektionen und Referenzen. Wichtig hierbei ist der skulpturale Raumbezug und weniger die reine Bildfläche als Widerspiegelung des Realen als Offenbarung des Imaginären ohne das Symbolische.

**Männer versus Frauen.** Hieraus folgernd eröffnen sich ausgehend vom Raum und der Gattung der Skulptur zwei zentrale Fragestellungen: zum einen zu unserer Positionierung im Raum und zum anderen zum Bild als imaginärer Folie der realen Gegenstände. In der Konzeption der Ausstellung waren seit 2012 verschiedene Parameter und diverse Konstellationen angedacht. Keinesfalls sollte es eine ikonografische Ausstellung werden, in der die Variationen der Verwendung von Spiegeln von einem gewissen Zeitpunkt an das Thema wäre. Vielmehr sollten die der Kunsthalle Düsseldorf entsprechenden Aufgaben in der Experimentierfreude und Orientierungssuche zeitgenössischer Fragestellungen – basierend auf einer Geschichte und Identität der Institution und des Kontexts – im Zentrum stehen. Mit Richter und seinem *Spiegel* in einer Nichtsammlung, der Dopplung und der Referentialität auf mannigfaltigen Ebenen gab es dann auch die wesentlichen Bezüge, die da wären: Düsseldorf und Köln, die spezifische Situation der Institution Kunsthalle seit 1966 (Eröffnung des neuen heutigen Gebäudes 1967) und das Jahr 1981, die Wechselbeziehungen zwischen dem Rheinland und Belgien, man denke nur an Marcel Broodthaers. Anfangs war die Ausstellung als diese Achsensymmetrie konzipiert, letztlich übrig geblieben ist die wichtigste Exponentin seit 1967, dem Eröffnungsjahr der Kunsthalle, Lili Dujourie. In ihrem Œuvre – wie in dem von Mucha – kommen alle Aspekte zum Tragen, die das Gerüst von *Schaf und Ruder / Wool and Water* widerspiegeln.[17]

In Werken **Lili Dujouries** vermittelt sich seit ihrer ersten Arbeit von 1967 ein Problemverständnis zwischen Form, Inhalt und Raum, zwischen strenger Konzeption und sinnlicher Materialität, Balance und Schwerkraft. Ihre Neuinterpretation von Themen, Formen und Gesten der Kunstgeschichte eröff-

history reveal an enormously precise oeuvre in various media. In addition to the two portraits—a granite box in which two concave mirrors provide a simultaneous view of our enlarged self, and a mirror that she shattered with the hammer—*Between Black and Pink* (1986) opens up an endless space as a cut in reality. In addition to the sculptures that allude to Minimalism, including her very first work from 1967 (cat. no. 1, like Richter's *Table*), the Belgian artist presents the wall-sized *Amerikaans Imperialisme [American Imperialism]* (1972), a contemporary commentary on art and politics (amid the Vietnam War and the bloody May Offensive by the RAF in Germany), which also formulates an enduring critique of the superficiality of the examination of both phenomena. The wall behind the steel plate is unpainted, a gap in reality, open like a window. The male-dominated "macho great art" of America is juxtaposed with a female counterpart.

Dujourie's sculptures have a convincing, conceptual stringency. They find refuge in the corner of a room, but their presence simultaneously searches for a way into other dimensions. Her work over the past fifty years shows manifold developments: from Minimalism and Arte Povera to video works in the 1970s to sculptures from the 1980s that radiate material beauty. There is also always a vision of theatricality that exudes glitz and glamor amid a world of illusions. With her sculptural formulation, the artist crosses the three-dimensional space that is an integral part of a construction, whether lying, leaning, standing, or hanging. How can a sculptural volume succeed that allows refuge and intimacy in space? This is Dujourie's main concern.

**Isa Genzken's** sculpture leans against the wall in a similarly lapidary manner to Dujourie's *Amerikaans Imperialisme [American Imperialism]*. Her *Large Window* (1988) stems from a specific suggestion for improvement as an architectural element for the facade of a gallery at Venloer Straße 21 in Cologne. Here the reflection of the window leaning against the wall becomes a membrane of a reality between inside and outside, similar to Dujourie's "gate." With this sculpture, Genzken turned against the facade designed by Oswald Mathias Ungers by suggesting that he replace one of the two square windows on the third floor. Genzken sought to improve what she saw as bad architecture with art for the opening of the building, which the architect did not understand and rejected because he simply did not understand anything about art.[18] The window was never installed, and instead was leaned against the wall at Galerie Buchholz as a reminder of the seriousness of architecture, as if it had been left there by chance, and ultimately it became a prototype of her artwork in many concrete references to architecture. Its form does not determine its planned function, but deconstructs the conventional function.

Works by two other female artists are exhibited between these two in the Upper Hall on the floor above (which also includes works by Rosemarie Trockel) and in the auditorium on the floor below: Elaine Sturtevant and **Astrid Klein.** In her sculptures and paintings since her studies at the Werkkunstschule in Cologne, Klein has dealt with pictures, text, and space, just as her early works from 1979 were created as material for collages based on the doubling of text and found photos. The political and feminist attitude in such "settings" is unmistakable! In the 1990s she also began creating transcendent neon sculptures as well as mirrors. Her works always have a bodily relationship to space, and even her photographs are conceived with space and architecture in mind. Since her scholarship in Paris, early on Klein began to use materials from the media:

net in unterschiedlichen Medien ein enorm präzises Œuvre. Neben den beiden Porträts – einem Granitkasten, in dem zwei Konkavspiegel einen gleichzeitigen Blick auf unser vergrößertes Selbst erlauben, und ein von ihr mit dem Hammer zertrümmerter Spiegel – eröffnet *Between Black and Pink* (1986) einen unendlichen Zwischenraum als metaphysischen Schnitt in der Realität. Neben drei auf die Minimal Art bezugnehmende Skulpturen, darunter ihre allererste Arbeit von 1967 (WVZ-Nummer 1 analog zu Richters *Tisch*), zeigt die Belgierin die wandfüllende Darlegung *Amerikaans Imperialisme [American Imperialism]* (1972), ein zeitgenössischer Kommentar zu Kunst und Politik (im Umfeld von Vietnamkrieg und blutiger Mai-Offensive der RAF in Deutschland), der zugleich eine fortwährende Kritik an der Oberflächlichkeit der Betrachtung beider Phänomene formuliert. Die Wand hinter der Stahlplatte ist unbemalt, ein Spalt in der Realität, offen wie ein Fenster. Der männlich dominierten „Machogroßkunst" Amerikas wird ein weibliches Pendant gegenübergestellt.

Dujouries Skulpturen sind von überzeugender, konzeptueller Stringenz. Sie finden Zuflucht in der Ecke eines Raums, aber ihre Präsenz sucht zugleich nach einem Weg in andere Dimensionen. Ihr Werk der letzten 50 Jahre zeigt mannigfaltige Entwicklungen: von der Minimal Art und Arte Povera zu Videoarbeiten in den 1970ern bis zu in stofflicher Schönheit erstrahlenden Skulpturen ab den 1980er-Jahren. Es ist auch immer die Vision einer Theaterrealität, die inmitten einer Welt des Scheins den Glitter und Glamour spüren lässt. Die Künstlerin übertritt mit skulpturalen Formulierungen den dreidimensionalen Raum, der integraler Bestandteil einer Konstruktion ist, ob liegend, lehnend, stehend oder hängend. Wie gelingt ein skulpturales Volumen, welches eine Zuflucht und Intimität im Raum ermöglicht? Das ist das Hauptanliegen von Dujourie.

Ebenso lapidar an der Wand wie die drei Stahlplatten in Dujouries *Amerikaans Imperialisme [American Imperialism]* lehnt die Skulptur von **Isa Genzken** an der Wand. Ihr *Großes Fenster* (1988) entstammt einem konkreten Verbesserungsvorschlag als architektonisches Element für eine Kölner Galeriehausfassade in der Venloer Straße 21. Hier wird die Spiegelung des an die Wand angelehnten Fensters analog zu Dujouries „Pforte" zu einer Membran einer Realität zwischen innen und außen, gleichwohl zum Bildträger und Konfliktfeld einer gestörten ästhetischen Befindlichkeit. Genzken wandte sich mit dieser „Skulptur" gegen den realisierten Fassadenentwurf von Oswald Mathias Ungers, indem sie ihm vorschlug, eines der beiden quadratischen Fenster der dritten Etage auszutauschen. Die nach Genzkens Ansicht schlechte Architektur sollte zur Eröffnung des Hauses mithilfe der Kunst verbessert werden, was der Raumdesigner jedoch nicht verstand und ablehnte, weil er eben von Kunst nichts verstand.[18] Montiert wurde das Fenster nie, sondern stattdessen als Mahnmal für den Ernst der Architektur in der Galerie Buchholz an die Wand gelehnt, als hätte man es dort zufällig vergessen, und letztlich zu einem Prototyp für ihr künstlerisches Schaffen in vielen konkreten Architekturbezügen. Die Form bestimmt nicht die geplante Funktion, sondern sie dekonstruiert die herkömmliche Funktion.

Zwischen diesen beiden Künstlerinnen finden sich zwei weitere auf den Ebenen Emporensaal (auch noch mit Rosemarie Trockel) oben und dem Kinosaal unten: Elaine Sturtevant und **Astrid Klein.** Klein beschäftigt sich in ihrem skulpturalen und bildnerischen Werk seit ihrem Studium an der Kölner Werkkunstschule mit Bild, Text und Raum, wie auch ihre frühe Arbeiten aus dem Jahre 1979 aufgrund der Dopplung von Text und gefundener Fotos als Material für Collagen entstanden. Die politische und feministische Haltung in derartigen „Settings" ist unverkennbar! Ab den 1990er-Jahren kamen transzendente Neonskulpturen hinzu, und dann auch Spiegel. Immer stehen ihre Werke in einem körperhaften Raumbezug, selbst die Fotoarbeiten sind raum- und architekturbezogen konzipiert. Seit ihrem Stipendium in Paris begann Klein früh, Pressematerialien einzusetzen:

> I am interested in political topics and the representation of women in the media and in film. Unlike in Germany, in France as well as Italy there was also the genre of the photographic novel, which was reflected in my works in the late seventies in the now well-known photo collages. Here I also made use of the tabloid media and film stills that deal with the portrayal of women and the power structures in these contexts.[19]

For instance, quotations from Antonin Artaud are printed on the ropes of the neon sculpture, and from Guy Debord on ribbons of text, and even the words "corriger la fortune" have numerous references ranging back to Gotthold Ephraim Lessing. The shots from this picture are aimed at shots in the mirror, which makes a direct appeal to or inclusion of the viewer unavoidable in all of Klein's works. In terms of the aesthetics of reception, the doublings, reflections, and references open up a space behind the visible level. Her shots in the mirror are the expression of desire and aggression about the inability to compose pictures behind the visible. The act of damaging the likeness simultaneously destroys it and "murders" the reflected room and the reflected self! Nonetheless, the wall is a wonderful, prismatically sparkling hall of mirrors à la Versailles.

Now let us turn to **Reinhard Mucha,** who used a drywall structure that was left over from the previous exhibition for his installation. Mucha weaves lived life and the work that maintains it as a daily effort into a material and conceptual foundation of past and present, art and life. The examination of this pair is based on knowledge, craftsmanship, and an understanding of materials; it becomes a mirror of both through the transformation by the artist. Dispositifs of showing are created. His works define being art as a certain form of being in a certain place and the contexts or events that determine these factors. Mucha resists the white cube and acts against and with it; he redefines the relationships in democratic terms. It is a relationship to power which he has formulated since 1981 with the display case sculpture *Der kluge Knecht* (2002) as the pictorial form of a rejection of rule and allegiance—the copy of his certificate from the master class at the Staatliche Kunstakademie Düsseldorf, certified by the Handwerkskammer Düsseldorf—and which he has since continued to propone.[20] The materiality calculated down to the smallest detail embodies institutional power, just as the institutional space of the museum represents an omnipotence, like the "footrests," these stand-ins that allow for an elevated perspective and have to do with "delusions of grandeur" and dismissal. Visual experiences have much to do with experience, and less with pure looking, today's "polyglot photo tourism: extravagantly wandering around," as Mucha once wrote, quoting Hans Magnus Enzensberger: "The tourist destroys what he seeks by finding it."

Mucha is constantly present in reflections or with footrests as the foundation of his work. He has always been interested in the bodily substrate in the counterpart or on it—a gesture of positioning against that of authority and power. The titles *MÄNNER FRAUEN* (1981) and *ODERIN* (1987) not only refer to two specific places, but semantic options in the world of semiotics. The specific arrangement leads to a reflection that shows an impenetrable (modern-day) gender debate, and in which a light ironically illuminates the work but offers little in the way of enlightenment. Nevertheless, the relationship to space and the concrete application of the problems of spatial experience and materialities are essential. Where does the viewer stand between the doubled sculptural elements and the reflected Suprematist abstract reverse glass painting, or between men and women? Between the work and him- or herself in the exhibition space? Mucha's selection of works and composition

> Politische Themen und die Darstellung der Frau in den Medien und im Film beschäftigten mich. Im Unterschied zu Deutschland gab es in Frankreich wie auch in Italien zudem das Genre des Fotoromans, was sich dann in meinen Arbeiten Ende der Siebziger, in den mittlerweile bekannten Fotocollagen spiegelte. Hier habe ich mich auch der Sensationspresse und der Filmstills bedient, die sich mit der Darstellung der Frau und den Machtstrukturen in diesen Gefügen beschäftigt.[19]

So ist auch in den anderen Werken Antonin Artaud auf den Seilen der Neonskulptur oder Guy Debord über Textbänder eingewoben, und sogar ein „corriger la fortune“ hat zahlreiche Referenzen bis zu Gotthold Ephraim Lessing. Die Schüsse aus diesem Bild zielen auf die Schüsse in die Spiegel, sodass in allen Werken Kleins eine direkte Ansprache oder Einbeziehung des Betrachters unvermeidbar wird. Rezeptionsästhetisch öffnet sie mit Dopplungen, Spiegeln und Referenzen einen Raum hinter der sichtbaren Ebene. Ihre Schüsse in den Spiegel sind Ausdruck von Lust und Aggression über das Unvermögen der Bildfindung hinter dem Sichtbaren. Die Verletzungen des Abbildes zerschlagen es zugleich und „morden“ den widergespiegelten Raum und das reflektierte Ich! Gleichwohl ist die Wand ein wunderschöner prismatisch funkelnder Spiegelsaal à la Versailles.

Betreten wir den Raum von **Reinhard Mucha,** der als Einziger aufgrund einer Trockenbauwand entstand, die von der Vorgängerausstellung erhalten geblieben ist. Mucha verwebt das gelebte Leben und die es erhaltende Arbeit als tägliches Bestreben zu einem materiellen wie ideellen Fundus von Historie und Gegenwart, von Kunst und Leben. Die Untersuchung dieses Paars basiert auf Kenntnis und Wissen, Handwerk und Materialkunde, sie wird zu einem Spiegel beider mittels der Transformation durch den Künstler. Es entstehen Dispositive des Zeigens. Seine Werke bestimmen das Kunstsein als bestimmte Seinsform an einem bestimmen Ort und der diese Faktoren bestimmenden Kontexte oder Begebenheiten. Mucha setzt sich gegen den White Cube zur Wehr, agiert gegen und mit ihm, definiert die Verhältnisse neu und demokratisch. Es ist ein Verhältnis zur Macht, welches er seit 1981 mit der Schaukastenskulptur *Der kluge Knecht* (2002) als bildhafte Form einer Absage an Herrschaft und Gefolgschaft formulierte – die von der Handwerkskammer Düsseldorf beglaubigte Kopie seines Meisterschülerbriefs der Staatlichen Kunstakademie Düsseldorfs – und seitdem fortwährend ins Feld führt.[20] Die bis in kleinste Detail kalkulierte Materialität verkörpert die institutionelle Wucht, wie auch der museale institutionelle Raum eine Allmacht darstellt. Wie die „Fußbänkchen“, die Stellvertreter, welche einen erhöhten Blickpunkt ermöglichen und mit „Größenwahn“ und Enthebung zu tun haben. Seherfahrungen haben eben viel mit Erfahrung zu tun, weniger mit dem reinen Schauen, dem heutigen „polyglotten Phototourismus: Aufwendig herumirren“, wie Mucha einmal schrieb und Hans Magnus Enzensberger zitierte: „Der Tourist zerstört das, was er sucht, indem er es findet.“

Mucha ist permanent in Spiegelungen oder mit Fußbänken als Fundament seines Schaffens zugegen. Immer schon beschäftigte ihn das körperliche Substrat im Gegenüber oder eben darauf. Eine Geste der Positionierung gegen die der Autorität und Macht. Mit den Worten *MÄNNER FRAUEN* (1981) und *ODERIN* (1987) sind nicht nur zwei bestimmte Orte gemeint, sondern semantische Optionen in der Welt der Zeichentheorien. Die spezifische Anordnung führt zu einer Spiegelung, die (heute) eine undurchdringliche Genderdebatte anzeigt und in der auch die zugehängte Lichtquelle augenzwinkernd zwar Licht, aber wenig Aufklärung bringt. Dennoch sind der Ortsbezug und die konkrete Anwendung der Fragestellungen von Raumerfahrungen und Materialitäten wesentlich. Wo steht der Betrachter zwischen den gedoppelten Skulpturenelementen und der gespiegelten suprematistischen Malereiabstraktion hinter Glas, wo zwischen Männer und Frauen? Zwischen dem Werk und sich im Ausstellungsraum? Muchas Werkauswahl und Komposition geht sensibel auf das Thema der Ausstellung ein, generiert im fein austarierten Einklang von Kunstwerken und deren

sensitively address the topic of the exhibition and generate questions about the our ability to gain insight in the context of showing in the finely balanced harmony of artworks and their materials.

Knowledge is and remains a dream of our existence. Since Plato's allegory of the cave, form, the shadow of things, has stood for their recognizable essence, which **Mischa Kuball** transforms into another media entity in his light projection. His work *Platon's Mirror* (2011) can be seen and experienced in precisely the dimensions of Richter's mirror in its usual location under the stairs at the Kunsthalle Düsseldorf. A mirror instead of Genzken's large window on the world? "Kuball does not refer to an already known position, but creates an experiment in order to illuminate anew our use of pictures in the most literal sense," Hans Belting writes.

> This is perhaps also why instead of Plato's cave it refers to Plato's mirror, in which we are meant to see ourselves. As paradoxical as it sounds, in Kuball's work we are not shown any images in the usual sense. They exist, but they come and go, so to speak, unnoticed and barely visible in the light that Kuball produces in the rooms—or, to be more precise, with devices. . . . One is tempted to call them 'light images' . . . . Thus, these are not images that are created in light, like photography, film, and the old slides, but ones that light up a room with the light of a projector that was actually built for displaying images. The second light source is the screen, which reflects the reflexes of the projected light with their light and shadow. Kuball uses not only a projection, but also a mirror world to produce light. . . . Once again we do not see what we normally expect from mirrors —pictures—even though they arrive there; instead, we perceive our environment with the light from mirrors. Kuball uses thin mirrored foils that move with the air currents as we walk through the room. They are mirrors with wrinkles, so to speak, in which shadows collect and light is refracted.[21]

Shadows of people (ideas) stage light and become mirrors of light. Plato's ideas are transformed into concrete shadow images, since if you come too close to the projection, you will cast a shadow. Kuball positioned a second "shadow" next to a projection under the stairs: the empty crate for Richter's mirror, simply leaning against the wall as a third leaning situation—in addition to Genzken's window and Dujourie's steel plates. The situation thus suggests a non-place, a transitory place, referring to Plato, and a very dark room devoid of light which does not allow any form of reflection.

In the doubling of the world behind the mirror lies a surprisingly concrete frame of reference for our questions about the real. In **Aron Mehzion's** works, facets of an endless imaginary space become palpable. His table installations, like experiments, show the intellectual pleasure in imagining a fourth dimension. Endless thought in the inverted double: in manifold possibilities the symbolic creates its own space that leads us behind the mirrors and back. The origin is that three-dimensional objects cannot be transferred into their own mirror image through casting and recasting processes.[22] Over twenty years ago, Mehzion had this experience as a student at the Kunstakademie Düsseldorf. Since then, he has examined this phenomenon in the wake of Duchamp, who explored the fourth dimension, and H. G. Wells, who brought his character Gottfried Plattner back from the fourth dimension in a mirror-image version of himself with his heart on the right side of his body. Cubism, Surrealism, Futurism, Suprematism, as well as Bauhaus and De Stijl dealt artistically with this conceptual model. With the proposal of a five-dimensional space-time—the Kaluza-Klein theory—the reality of a multidimensional space continues

Materialien die Fragen nach der Erkenntnisfähigkeit im Kontext des Zeigens.

Erkenntnis ist und bleibt ein Traum unseres Daseins. Seit Platons Höhlengleichnis steht die Form, der Schatten der Dinge, für ihre erkennbare Wesenheit, was **Mischa Kuball** in seiner Lichtprojektion zu einer weiteren medialen Entität transformiert. Seine Arbeit *'platon's spiegel'* bewegt sich exakt in der Dimension von Richters *Spiegel* und ist an dessen jahrelang angestammtem Platz unter der Treppe in der Kunsthalle zu sehen und zu erfahren. Ein Spiegel statt wie bei Genzken ein großes Fester zur Welt? „Kuball beruft sich nicht auf eine bereits bekannte Position, sondern stellt eine Versuchsanordnung her, um unseren Umgang mit Bildern im wörtlichsten Sinne neu zu beleuchten", schreibt Hans Belting.

> Deswegen ist vielleicht auch nicht von „Platons Höhle" die Rede, sondern von Platons Spiegel, in dem wir uns selbst sehen sollen. So paradox es klingt, bekommen wir in Kuballs Arbeit gar keine Bilder im üblichen Sinne zu sehen. [...] Man ist versucht, von „Lichtbildern" zu reden, wenn man den alten Begriff neu fasst. Es sind demgemäß keine Bilder, die im Licht entstehen, wie die Fotografie, der Film und das alte Diapositiv, sondern solche, welche mit dem Licht eines Projektors, der eigentlich für eine Bildübertragung gebaut wurde, einen Raum ausleuchten. Die zweite Lichtquelle ist der Screen, der die Reflexe des Projektionslichts mit ihrem Licht und Schatten zurückwirft. Kuball benutzt nicht nur die Projektion, sondern auch eine Spiegelwelt, um Licht zu erzeugen. [...] Wieder sehen wir nicht das, was wir gewöhnlich von Spiegeln erwarten, also Bilder, wenngleich sie dort ankommen, sondern wir nehmen unsere Umgebung mit dem Licht aus Spiegeln wahr. Kuball nutzt dünne Spiegelfolien, die sich mit dem Luftzug und mit unseren Schritten im Raum bewegen. Es sind, wenn man so will, Spiegel, die Falten werfen, in denen sich Schatten sammeln und sich das Licht bricht.[21]

Schatten von Menschen (den Ideen) inszenieren das Licht, werden zu Spiegeln des Lichts. Die Ideen Platons verwandeln sich zu konkreten Schattenbildern, denn wer der Projektion zu nahe tritt, wirft Schatten. Neben der Projektion unter der Treppe hat Kuball einen zweiten „Schatten" positioniert: die leere Transportkiste des Richter-Spiegels, anspruchslos an die Wand gelehnt als dritte gelehnte Situation – neben Genzkens Fenster und Dujouries Stahlplatten. Die Situation deutet somit einen Nichtort an, einen transitorischen Ort, sich auf Platon beziehend, und einen sehr dunklen, lichttoten Raum, der keine Form einer Spiegelung erlaubt.

In der Verdopplung der Welt hinter dem Spiegel liegt ein überraschend konkreter Referenzrahmen für unsere Fragen an das Reale. In den Arbeiten von **Aron Mehzion** werden Facetten eines unendlichen Denkraums erfahrbar. Seine Tischinstallationen zeigen, Versuchsanordnungen gleich, das intellektuelle Vergnügen am Imaginären einer vierten Dimension. Unendliches Denken im seitenverkehrten Doppel: In mannigfaltigen Möglichkeiten verschafft sich das Symbolische einen eigenen Raum, welcher uns hinter die Spiegel und wieder zurückführt. Ursprung ist, dass sich dreidimensionale Objekte nicht durch Ab- und Umgussverfahren in ihr eigenes Spiegelbild überführen lassen.[22] Diese Erfahrung machte Mehzion bereits vor über 20 Jahren als Student an der Kunstakademie Düsseldorf. Seitdem erforscht er dieses Phänomen auf den Spuren Duchamps, der die vierte Dimension erkundete, und H.G. Wells', der seine Figur Gottfried Plattner spiegelverkehrt und mit dem Herzen in der rechten Körperhälfte aus der vierten Dimension zurückkehren ließ. Kubismus, Surrealismus, Futurismus, Suprematismus, aber auch Bauhaus und De Stijl haben sich mit diesem Denkmodell künstlerisch auseinandergesetzt. Mit dem Vorschlag einer fünfdimensionalen Raumzeit – der Kaluza-Klein-Theorie – lebt die Realität eines mehrdimensionalen Raums in den Modellen von Supergravitation und Superstringtheorie der aktuellen Physik fort. Mehzion nutzt das digitale 3-D-Druckverfahren für seine Werkserie, die sich – vielleicht erstmals seit Duchamp – auf grundsätzliche Weise mit einer vierdimensionalen Perspektive befasst, und verwendet halb transparente Spiegel. Falk Wolf beschreibt dies folgendermaßen:

today in the models of supergravity and superstring theory. Mehzion uses 3D printing for his series of works, which—perhaps for the first time since Duchamp—fundamentally deal with a four-dimensional perspective, and uses half-transparent mirrors. Falk Wolf writes the following:

> Placed between two mirror-image figures, they allow perfect overlaps or penetrations of the reflection of one figure with the view to the other. The surface of the mirror thus offers a view that reflects and also penetrates. In interaction with the sculptures, this means that one hand is both a left and a right hand. This is not an oscillating or switching of one possibility into another, but an irresolvable fusing of the objects into a single picture that is perceptible at any moment and from whatever perspective it is viewed. The arm that is missing from one of the sculptures is both there and not there in the mirror, and it is simultaneously a right arm and a left arm. Aron Mehzion's mirrors show a world that cannot be entered, but which is nonetheless present in the realm of the possible in physics and mathematics. His large-scale drawings on anodized aluminum are very similar. They consist of iterations of drawn shapes, each of which refers to something physical, but whose repetition brings about the dissolution of the physical. They also hint at a perspective, dissolve surface and form, and challenge perception.[23]

In this regard, the works of the American artist **Sturtevant** tie in with and supplement the questions in Mehzion's work as well as Richter's. Her works generally stand for the complex of reflections, doublings, and references. Beginning in 1964, Sturtevant turned the concept of artistic originality on its head by not producing a single original, but proceeding by appropriation: selective doubling and faithful reflecting of the original. Her works in the exhibition—copying the most important representatives of Conceptual Art, Duchamp and Robert Gober—circle back to the starting point. Duchamp's *Nude Descending a Staircase* (1912), Man Ray's Hermes portrait (1966) and *Adam and Eve* (1967), and Gober's penis and vagina designs for his tapestries (1994) stand for (men and women and) the origin and reflection of the world (or humanity) and thus also for the beginning of narcissism. Or, the crucial question would be, could we live without mirrors? Nevertheless, these works have not only feminist or Freudian backgrounds; with Gober, Sturtevant focuses more on the obsession of art (and culture) with physical surfaces. Our identity is mainly shaped by our (dysfunctional) relationship to our own body and to others' bodies. Sturtevant as a master of this concept was also knowledgeable about crowd psychology. She physically dissected the extreme brutality of contemporary pop culture. Today, in the age of selfie sticks, Sturtevant would find no shortage of material. As a continuous principle of the concrete double materiality, she allows us to precisely rethink the uncertain intermediate space (the break or gap in reality) that, in her own words, "leads to a loss of balance that continually spurs one to think."

**Rosemarie Trockel** conceived a wall with two works for the Upper Hall which oppose one another, so to speak. Personal motifs and references of a first-person narrative are interwoven with personal references in *Cluster I – Bachelor's Luck* (2015), a twenty-two-part collage set. This is joined by a playful "breathing body" as a counterpart to the ego with the wonderful title *My Generation, No Meat* (2000). Trockel alludes to our desires and drives and presents us with wish machines à la Duchamp, in which she reveals our desire for knowledge as well as the impossibility of gaining this knowledge. Tellingly, a "self-portrait" is part of the collage—next to the photograph in a bull-fighting arena—which shows a view of the mirror between her thighs, the "origin of

Zwischen zwei spiegelsymmetrische Figuren gestellt, erlauben sie perfekte Überlagerungen oder Durchdringungen des Spiegelbildes der einen mit der Durchsicht auf die andere Figur. Die Oberfläche des Spiegels gewährt so einen Blick, der sowohl reflektiert als auch durchdringt. Im Zusammenspiel mit den Skulpturen ergibt es sich, dass eine Hand zugleich eine linke und eine rechte Hand ist. Dies ist kein Oszillieren oder Umschlagen der einen in die andere Möglichkeit, sondern eine in jedem Betrachtungsmoment und aus jedem Betrachtungswinkel wahrnehmbare, unlösbare Verschmelzung der Gegensätze zu einem Bild. Der Arm, der bei der einen Skulptur fehlt, ist im Spiegel zugleich da und nicht da, und er ist zugleich ein rechter und ein linker Arm. Die Spiegel von Aron Mehzion lassen eine nicht betretbare Welt aufscheinen, die aber dennoch in den Möglichkeitsräumen von Physik und Mathematik präsent ist. Seine großformatigen Zeichnungen auf eloxiertem Aluminium sind ihnen sehr ähnlich. Sie bestehen aus iterierenden zeichnerischen Formen, die sich zwar jede für sich auf Gegenständliches beziehen, in der Wiederholung aber die Auflösung des Gegenständlichen betreiben. Auch sie deuten eine Perspektive an, lösen Fläche und Form auf und fordern die Wahrnehmung heraus.[23]

Insofern sind die Werke der Amerikanerin **Sturtevant** eine Kopplung und analoge Ergänzung zu den Fragestellungen bei Mehzion, aber auch bei Richter. Ihre Werke stehen generell für den Komplex der Spiegelungen, Vedopplungen und Referenzen. Sturtevant stellte ab 1964 zeitlebens das Konzept künstlerischer Originalität auf den Kopf, indem sie kein einziges Original herstellte, sondern rein appropriativ vorging: selektive Verdopplung und originalgetreue Spiegelung des Originals. Mit ihren Werken in der Ausstellung – die wichtigsten Vertreter der Konzeptkunst, Duchamp und Robert Gober kopierend – schließt sich der Kreis. Duchamps *Akt, eine Treppe herabsteigend,* das „Hermes"-Porträt (1966) und *Adam und Eva* (1967), beide von Man Ray, sowie von Gober die Penis- und Vaginaentwürfe für seine Wandtapeten (1994) stehen für („Männer / Frauen" und) den Ursprung und die Widerspiegelung der Welt (oder der Menschheit) und damit auch für den Beginn des Narziss(-mus). Oder, so würde die entscheidende Frage lauten, könnten wir ohne Spiegel leben? Gleichwohl haben diese Werke nicht allein feministische oder freudianische Hintergründe, Sturtevant zeigt vor allem mit Gober eher die Obsessivität von Kunst (und Kultur) gegenüber physischen Oberflächen. Unsere Identität ist hauptsächlich geprägt von unserem (gestörten) Verhältnis zum eigenen Körper und zu dem der anderen. Sturtevant als Meisterin des Konzepts war zugleich eine Kennerin der Massenpsychologie. Die extreme Brutalität der zeitgenössischen Popkultur wurde von ihr körperlich seziert. Heute, im Zeitalter von Selfies an langen Stangen, hätte Sturtevant viel zu tun. Als ein durchgehendes Prinzip über die konkrete Dopplermaterialität lässt sie uns exakt den unbestimmten Zwischenraum (den Schnitt oder Spalt in der Realität) neu denken, der, so sagte sie selbst, „zu einem Gleichgewichtsverlust führt, der das Denken immer vorantreibt."

**Rosemarie Trockel** konzipierte für den Emporensaal eine Wand mit zwei Arbeiten, die sich sozusagen gegenüberstehen. Persönliche Motive und Referenzen einer Ich-Erzählung sind in *Cluster I – Bachelor's Luck* (2015), einem 22-teiligen Collageset mit persönlichen Referenzen verwoben. Hinzu gesellt sich ein spielerischer „atmender Körper" als Gegenüber des Egos mit dem wundervollen Titel *My Generation, No Meat* (2000). Trockel spielt auf unsere Begehren und Triebe an und präsentiert uns zwei in gewisser Weise Wunschmaschinen à la Duchamp, in denen sie unser Verlangen nach Erkenntnis und gleichzeitig die Unmöglichkeit, diese Erkenntnis auch zu erlangen, offenlegt. Bezeichnenderweise gehört ein „Selbstporträt" zur Collage – neben der Fotografie in einer Stierkampfarena –, das ihren unsichtbaren Blick in den Spiegel zwischen ihre Schenkel, den „Ursprung der Welt" wiedergibt. Somit werden wir am Ende wieder auf uns selbst zurückgeworfen. Der phallische Sack, mal schlaff herabhängend, mal steif aufgerichtet, ist nur mit Luft gefüllt – ein Ventilator pumpt diese rhythmisch hinein. Kein Fleisch. Reine Hülle, Form! Meine Generation.

the world." Thus we are ultimately once again forced to rely on ourselves. The phallic bag, sometimes hanging limply, at others erect, is only filled with air—a fan pumps it in rhythmically. No meat. Pure surface, form! My generation. Or is the wall once again a symbol for men and women? The search for meaning begins again. Never-ending and usually in the morning with a glimpse in the mirror—by men as well as women, equally.

**Afterword.** The work of all of the artists chosen for this exhibition deals with spatial and sculptural thought, a sculptural forming, a mental and physical enormously aesthetic plasticity that encompasses psychological, political, or social, even philosophical frames of reference. The selection of the works was deliberately limited in order to precisely direct their interaction with the architecture of the museum and not to create a mirror world exhibition. On the contrary: the mirror as a vehicle and symbol is meant to offer food for thought, and by no means exhaustive answers. The aesthetic interaction of the nine artists stems solely from the added value of a referential context of the works which reveals its own special quality in the experience of space.

The timeframe of the works in the exhibition spans exactly half a century and thus alludes to the fiftieth birthday of the Kunsthalle Düsseldorf as an institution, which was reborn on 30 April 1967 and moved to the fantastic building on Grabbeplatz. The oldest work in the exhibition is from 1966, now exactly fifty years ago; Sturtevant's *Adam and Eve* is from 1967, as are both of Dujourie's works, numbers 1 and 4 in her catalogue raisonné. In the Upper Hall, these two works show a perfect symbiosis of artworks and architecture in an impressive interaction with *Amerikaans Imperialisme [American Imperialism]* and the works by Klein and Trockel on either side on the walls. Of course, Genzken's attack on Ungers's architecture in Cologne also has a reflection and a reference in Düsseldorf with the Museum Kunstpalast.[24] And it is precisely this that is the political and social element of the exhibition *Schaf und Ruder / Wool and Water* at the Kunsthalle Düsseldorf and beyond. The Kunsthalle Düsseldorf is the most suitable exhibition venue in Düsseldorf, which—if you ask artists—has to do with proportions and aesthetics as well as independence and autonomy. This must not be jeopardized, especially in a political time in which the uncertainty about the present is taken advantage of by populist propaganda in the urban context. "Culture is the DNA of a city. Here cultural heritage meets contemporary art and culture," the German Commission for UNESCO writes. "Together they are the heartbeat of the continued development of cities and innovation. In cities people come together to exchange ideas, create new things, and be productive. Cities are drivers of human development."[25] In a time when art and culture are considered hard economic factors, an urban identity consists of meaningless constructions of pure cement and steel, and social decline and disintegration are palpable, culture needs to be protected as an existential sustenance for people, since it revolves around them as the measure of all things.

And so, in the coming year we will hold up a mirror to ourselves, bearing in mind its cultural heritage.

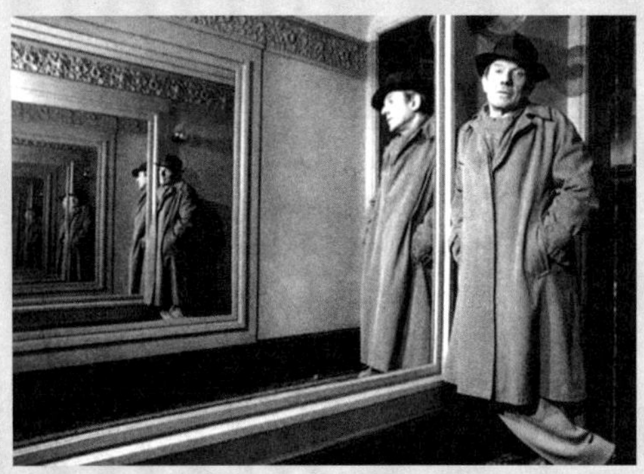

11

Oder ist diese Wand doch auch wieder ein Sinnbild für Männer / Frauen? Die Sinnsuche beginnt erneut. Permanent und meist morgens mit dem Blick in den Spiegel – von Männern wie Frauen, egal.

**Nachwort.** Bei allen für diese Ausstellung ausgewählten Künstlerinnen und Künstlern geht es um ein dezidiert räumlich-plastisches Denken, um eine bildnerische Ausformung, eine mentale wie reale enorm ästhetische Plastizität bis hin zu psychologischen, politischen oder sozialen, auch philosophischen Bezugsrahmen. Die Auswahl der Werke wurde bewusst reduziert, um ihr Zusammenspiel mit der Architektur der Kunsthalle enorm präzise auszurichten und keinesfalls eine ikonografische Spiegelweltenaussstellung einzurichten. Im Gegenteil, der Spiegel als Vehikel und Sinnbild soll eigene Denkanstöße geben, keinesfalls sich erschöpfende Antworten. Im ästhetischen Zusammenspiel der neun Künstlerinnen und Künstler ist allein der Mehrwert eines referentiellen Werkezusammenhangs gegeben, der im räumlichen Erleben seine ganz besondere Qualität aufscheinen lässt.

Der Zeitrahmen der Werke in der Ausstellung umfasst exakt ein halbes Jahrhundert und verweist somit auch auf den 50. Geburtstag der Kunsthalle Düsseldorf als Institution, welche am 30. April 1967 neu geboren und in das großartige Haus am Grabbeplatz einzog. Von 1966, eben nun vor genau 50 Jahren, ist die älteste Arbeit in der Ausstellung, von Sturtevant, *Adam und Eva* stammt von 1967, ebenso die beiden Arbeiten von Dujourie, in ihrem Werkverzeichnis die Nummern 1 und 4. Diese beiden Arbeiten zeigen im Emporensaal in beeindruckendem Zusammenspiel mit *Amerikaans Imperialisme [American Imperialism]* und den flankierenden Werken an den Wänden von Klein und Trockel eine perfekte Symbiose von Kunstwerken und Architektur. Genzkens Kölner Attacke gegen Ungers' Architektur hat in Düsseldorf mit dem Museum Kunstpalast natürlich ebenfalls eine Spiegelung und Referenz.[24] Genau das ist auch das politische und soziale Moment in der Ausstellung *Schaf und Ruder / Wool and Water* in der Kunsthalle und darüber hinaus. Die Kunsthalle ist das geeignetste Ausstellungshaus in Düsseldorf, was – wenn man vor allem die Künstlerinnen und Künstler fragt – Proportionen und Ästhetik angeht und was Unabhängigkeit und Autonomie betrifft. Dies darf nicht gefährdet werden, gerade in einer politischen Zeit, welche die Unsicherheit des Zeitgenössischen als populistische Meinungsmache im urbanen Kontext leichtfertig aufs Spiel setzt. „Kultur ist die DNA einer Stadt. Kulturelles Erbe trifft hier auf zeitgenössische Kunst und Kultur“, schreibt aktuell die Deutsche UNESCO-Kommission. „Zusammen sind sie der Herzschlag urbaner Weiterentwicklung und Innovation. In Städten kommen Menschen zusammen, um sich auszutauschen, Neues zu kreieren und produktiv zu sein. Städte sind Treiber menschlicher Entwicklung.“[25] In einer Zeit, in der Kunst und Kultur als harte Wirtschaftsfaktoren bewertet werden, eine urbane Identität in nichtssagende Konstruktionen aus puren Beton und Stahl aufgeht, sozialer Niedergang und gesellschaftlicher Zerfall deutlicher spürbar sind, muss Kultur als existenzieller Nährboden für den Menschen geschützt werden, da sie ihn selbst als das Maß aller Dinge ins Zentrum stellt.

Im nächsten Jahr dann halten wir uns eingedenk des kulturellen Erbes selbst den Spiegel vor.

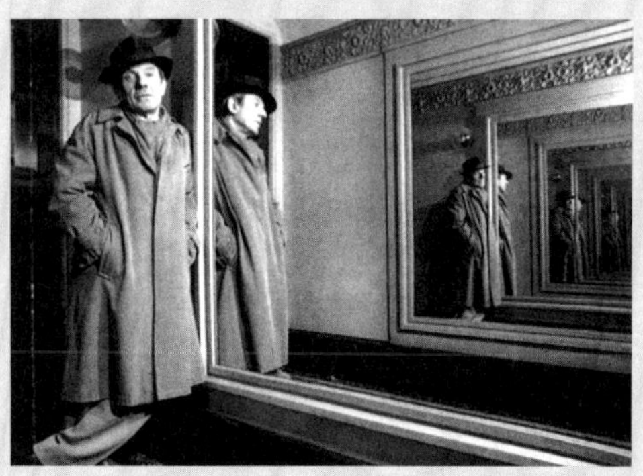

**11 Gilles Deleuze**

**1** The film is based on the book *Do Androids Dream of Electric Sheep?* by Philip K. Dick (1968). Also cf. the relationship to the Other and Jacques Lacan's mirror stage in: Klaus Benesch, "Technology, Art, and the Cybernetic Body: The Cyborg as Cultural Other in Fritz Lang's 'Metropolis' and Philip K. Dick's 'Do Androids Dream of Electric Sheep?'," *Amerikastudien/American Studies 44 (3 Body/Art),* 1999, pp. 379–392.

**2** On the mirror as a paradigm for interpreting the world, cf. Thomas Mießgang, "Die Pforte der Wahrnehmung," in: exh. cat. Belvedere Museum Vienna, 2014, *Die andere Seite: Spiegel und Spiegelungen in der zeitgenössischen Kunst,* ed. Agnes Husslein-Arco et al., Vienna, 2014, pp. 21–34.

**3** In 2013 the Kunsthalle Düsseldorf devoted an exhibition to this subject entitled *Living with Pop: A Reproduction of Capitalist Realism,* which was also shown in 2014 at Artists Space in New York.

**4** Doris Krystof, "Visuelle Spekulationen: Spiegel und Glas bei Gerhard Richter," in: exh. cat. Museum Franz Gertsch, Burgdorf, *Gerhard Richter ohne Farbe,* ed. Reinhard Spieler, Ostfildern-Ruit, 2005, pp. 78–85.

**5** Exh. cat. Kunsthalle Düsseldorf, 1981, *Georg Baselitz, Gerhard Richter,* Düsseldorf, 1981, n.p.

**6** Cf. exh. cat. Kunsthalle Düsseldorf, *Gerhard Richter: Bilder 1962–1985,* ed. Jürgen Harten, Cologne, 1986, p. 242.

**7** The publication *Gerhard Richter: Acht Grau* as well as the corresponding exhibition deal with a commission for the Deutsche Guggenheim Berlin consisting of eight monumental mirrored panels. Referring back to a work from the 1960s, the blurred reflections of the painted glass panels in this work point to a confused, complex nature of reality. With these panels, Richter questions art's endeavor to capture reality or its fleetingness. Cf. https://www.gerhard-richter.com/de/literature/catalogues/solo-exhibitions/gerhard-richter-acht-grau-83 (accessed on 28 Oct. 2016).

**8** Outside the English-speaking world, Humpty Dumpty is primarily known from his appearance in Lewis Carroll's *Through the Looking-Glass* (1871), where Alice discusses semantics with him. "Humpty Dumpty" can also be used in English to refer to a short, round person. Sometimes it serves as a synonym for something breakable that cannot be repaired or would be very difficult to repair.

**9** Dieter E. Zimmer: Lewis Caroll – Alice im Wunderland, in: *DIE ZEIT* (2 May 1980): "Alice must suddenly prove herself in a world whose rules she does not yet know and which seem simply absurd to her. She has learned that etiquette is incredibly important; at first, though, this is terribly difficult for her to understand. This wonderland is surely full of reflections of her Victorian bourgeois childhood: tedious grammar lessons, tea parties, croquet games, grinning cats, long summer afternoons on sunny lawns. But it is shot through with more than a hint of adult life in which, they say, people are judged and beheaded."

**10** Many thanks to David Gray and Rüdiger Schöttle for information on the installation.

**11** The reference to the 1988 exhibition *Freeze* in London with Damien Hirst and other artists in an allusion to Saatchi's first gallery seems interesting to me.

**12** Hans-Joachim Maaz, *Die narzisstische Gesellschaft: Ein Psychogramm,* Munich, 2012.

**13** Cf. for example exh. cat. Belvedere Museum Vienna, 2014, *Die andere Seite* (see note 2) or *Man in the Mirror,* Vanhaerents Art Collection, Brussels, 3 May 2014 – 28 Oct. 2017.

**14** "I want to build a new space, a space without a beginning or an end, in which everything lives and is brought to life, which is simultaneously quiet and

1 Der Film basiert auf dem Buch von Philip K. Dick, *Do Androids Dream of Electric Sheep?*, 1968. Vgl. hierzu auch die Beziehung zum großen Anderen und Jacques Lacans Spiegelstadium in: Klaus Benesch, Technology, Art, and the Cybernetic Body: The Cyborg as Cultural Other in Fritz Lang's "Metropolis" and Philip K. Dick's "Do Androids Dream of Electric Sheep?", *Amerikastudien/American Studies 44 (3 Body/Art)*, 1999, S. 379–392.

2 Zum Spiegel als Paradigma der Weltdeutung vgl. Thomas Mießgang, Die Pforte der Wahrnehmung, in: Ausst.-Kat. Belvedere Wien 2014, *Die andere Seite. Spiegel und Spiegelungen in der zeitgenössischen Kunst*, hrsg. von Agnes Husslein-Arco u. a., Wien 2014, S. 21–34.

3 Diesem Themenfeld widmete 2013 die Kunsthalle Düsseldorf die Ausstellung *Leben mit Pop. Eine Reproduktion des Kapitalistischen Realismus*, die 2014 auch im Artists Space in New York zu sehen war.

4 Doris Krystof, Visuelle Spekulationen. Spiegel und Glas bei Gerhard Richter, in: Ausst.-Kat. Museum Franz Gertsch, Burgdorf, *Gerhard Richter ohne Farbe*, hrsg. von Reinhard Spieler, Ostfildern-Ruit 2005, S. 78–85.

5 Ausst.-Kat. Kunsthalle Düsseldorf 1981, *Georg Baselitz Gerhard Richter*, Düsseldorf 1981, o. S.

6 Vgl. Ausst.-Kat. Kunsthalle Düsseldorf, *Gerhard Richter. Bilder 1962–1985*, hrsg. von Jürgen Harten, Köln 1986, S. 242.

7 Die Publikation *Gerhard Richter. Acht Grau* wie auch die dazugehörige Ausstellung beschäftigen sich mit einer Auftragsarbeit für die Deutsche Guggenheim Berlin, die aus acht monumentalen verspiegelten Tafeln besteht. Zurückgreifend auf eine Arbeit aus den 1960er-Jahren verweist dieses Werk durch die verschwommene Spiegelung der bemalten Glastafeln auf eine verworrene, komplexe Beschaffenheit der Realität. Das Bemühen der Kunst, die Realität bzw. ihre Flüchtigkeit zu bannen, wird mit diesen Tafeln von Richter infrage gestellt. Vgl. https://www.gerhard-richter.com/de/literature/catalogues/solo-exhibitions/gerhard-richter-acht-grau-83 (abgerufen am 28.10.2016).

8 Humpty Dumpty ist eine Figur aus einem britischen Kinderreim, ein menschenähnliches Ei. Im englischen Sprachraum ist dieser Kinderreim seit Jahrhunderten populär und so etwas wie ein fester Bestandteil der Sammlung von Kinderreimen in *Mother Goose*. Außerhalb des englischen Sprachraums wurde Humpty Dumpty vor allem durch Lewis Carroll in *Alice hinter den Spiegeln* (1871) bekannt, wo er mit Alice über Semantik diskutiert. Als „Humpty Dumpty" bezeichnen englische Muttersprachler aber auch eine kleine rundliche Person. Hin und wieder dient der Name auch als Synonym für etwas Zerbrechliches, das man nicht oder nur schwer wieder reparieren kann.

9 Dieter E. Zimmer: Lewis Caroll – Alice im Wunderland, in: DIE ZEIT vom 02.05.1980: „Alice hat sich unversehens in einer Welt zu bewähren, deren Spielregeln sie noch nicht kann und die ihr vorerst auch schlechterdings absurd erscheinen. Sie hat gelernt, daß Etikette schrecklich wichtig ist; zunächst scheint ihr diese aber vor allem schrecklich unverständlich. Wohl ist dieses Wunderland noch voller Reflexe ihrer viktorianischen großbürgerlichen Kinderwelt: ungeliebte Grammatikstunden, Teegesellschaften, Krockettspiele, fröhliche Katzen, lange Sommernachmittage auf sonnigem Rasen, aber es ist durchschossen von mehr als einer Ahnung des Erwachsenenlebens, in dem, hört man, gerichtet und geköpft wird."

10 Für Hinweise zur Installation danke ich herzlich David Gray und Rüdiger Schöttle.

11 Interessant erscheint mir der Hinweis auf die im Juli 1988 in London realisierte Ausstellung *Freeze* von Damien Hirst und anderen Künstlern in Anspielung auf Saatchis erste Galerie.

12 Hans-Joachim Maaz, *Die narzisstische Gesellschaft. Ein Psychogramm*, München 2012.

13 Vgl. z. B. Ausst.-Kat. Belvedere Wien 2014, *Die andere Seite.* Wie Anm. 2 oder *Man in the Mirror*, Vanhaerents Art Collection, Brüssel, 03.05.2014–28.10.2017.

14 „Ich will einen neuen Raum bauen, einen Raum ohne Anfang und Ende, in dem alles lebt und zum Leben aufgefor-

loud, still and in motion.... If you hold a mirror to a mirror, you will find an endless, boundless space with unlimited possibilities, a new metaphysical space." Christian Megert, *EIN NEUER RAUM,* 1961.

**15** Cf. on this complex topic Marshall McLuhan, "The Gadget Lover: Narcissus as Narcosis," in: Marshall McLuhan, *Understanding Media: The Extensions of Man,* Cambridge, 1964, pp. 41–47.

**16** From an e-mail to the author on 13 Oct. 2016: "*Self-Begotten* deals with the origin of all things. Where there is no second part, there can only be a self-creating system. In a process of self-knowledge of the striving to duplicate oneself."

**17** Three women from Cologne are juxtaposed with three men from Düsseldorf, Richter between them, then Dujourie in Belgium and Sturtevant from Paris to the United States.

**18** In the first presentation in 1988, Genzken and Ungers's correspondence was exhibited, as Daniel Buchholz recounted to me.

**19** Astrid Klein in an interview with Birgit Sonna on 31 Jan. 2013 for *art:* http://www.art-magazin.de/kunst/12454-rtkl-astrid-klein-berlin-bilder-sollen-sich-im-kopf-einbrennen (accessed on 28 Oct. 2016).

**20** The Clever Servant (Ohne Titel – Staatliche Kunstakademie – Düsseldorf – 1981), 2002. Here with the fairy tale by the Brothers Grimm and a personal anecdote.

**21** Hans Belting, „Plato's Shadow Images in Video Light," in: exh. cat. ZKM, Karlsruhe, 2012; *Mischa Kuball: Platon's Mirror and the Actuality oft he Cave Allegory,* ed. Andreas Beitin, Leonhard Emmerling, Blair French, Cologne, 2012, pp. 21–25.

**22** Cf. here and in the following the text by Falk Wolf at: http://www.danielmarzona.com/exhibitions/inverresion/text/ (accessed on 20 Oct. 2016).

**23** Falk Wolf, ibid.

**24** The new architectural concept for the Ehrenhof complex in Düsseldorf, especially the Kunstpalast including the Robert-Schumann-Saal and an office building for E.ON AG, was designed by Oswald Mathias Ungers and realized through the public-private partnership of the city of Düsseldorf and E.ON AG before the opening in September 2001. Cf. http://www.smkp.de/ueber-uns/geschichte/geschichte-architektur/ (accessed on 28 Oct. 2016).

**25** Prof. Dr. Karin von Welck, German Commission for UNESCO, 18 Oct. 2016, https://www.unesco.de/kultur/2016/unesco-weltbericht-kultur-urbane-zukunft.html. This year's global conference on housing and urban development, *Habitat III* (17–20 Oct. 2016 in Quito, Ecuador) is a central instrument for the implementation of the 2030 Agenda for Sustainable Development.

dert wird, der gleichzeitig ruhig und laut, unbewegt und bewegt ist. […] Wenn Sie einen Spiegel gegen einen Spiegel halten, finden Sie einen Raum ohne Ende und Grenzen, einen Raum mit unbeschränkten Möglichkeiten, einen neuen metaphysischen Raum." Christian Megert, *EIN NEUER RAUM,* 1961.

**15** Vgl. zu diesem komplexen Themenfeld u. a.: Marshall McLuhan, Verliebt in seine Apparate. Narzissmus als Narkose, in: Ders., *Die magischen Kanäle. Understanding Media,* Düsseldorf/Wien 1968, S. 50–57.

**16** Aus einer E-Mail an den Autor vom 13.10.2016: „Self-Begotten (sich selbst erschaffen) handelt vom Ursprung aller Dinge. Wo es kein zweites gibt, kann es nur ein sich selbst erschaffendes System geben. In einem Prozess der Selbsterkenntnis hinstrebenden Verdoppelung des eigenen Selbst."

**17** 3 Frauen aus Köln stehen 3 Männern aus Düsseldorf gegenüber, Richter dazwischen, dann Dujourie in Belgien und mit Sturtevant über Paris bis in die USA.

**18** In der Erstpräsentation 1988 wurde der Schriftwechsel zwischen Genzken und Ungers ausgestellt, wie mir Daniel Buchholz schilderte.

**19** Astrid Klein im Interview mit Birgit Sonna am 31.01.2013 für art: http://www.art-magazin.de/kunst/12454-rtkl-astrid-klein-berlin-bilder-sollen-sich-im-kopf-einbrennen (abgerufen am 28.10.2016).

**20** Der kluge Knecht (Ohne Titel – Staatliche Kunstakademie – Düsseldorf – 1981), 2002. Hier mit dem Märchen der Gebrüder Grimm und einer persönlichen Anekdote.

**21** Hans Belting, Platons Schattenbilder im Video-Licht, in: Ausst.-Kat. ZKM Karlsruhe, Karlsruhe 2012; *Mischa Kuball: Platons Spiegel und die Aktualität des Höhlengleichnisses,* hrsg. von Andreas Beitin, Leonhard Emmerling und Blair French, Köln 2012, S. 21–25.

**22** Vgl. hier und im Folgenden den Text von Falk Wolf unter: http://www.danielmarzona.com/exhibitions/inverresion/text/ (abgerufen am 20.10.2016).

**23** Falk Wolf, ebd.

**24** Die architektonische Neukonzeption des Düsseldorfer Ehrenhof-Komplexes, insbesondere des Kunstpalastes einschließlich des Robert-Schumann-Saals und eines Bürogebäudes für die E.ON AG, wurde nach einem Wettbewerb von dem Kölner Architekten Oswald Mathias Ungers entworfen und durch die Public-Private-Partnership der Stadt Düsseldorf und der E.ON AG bis zur Eröffnung im September 2001 umgesetzt. Vgl. http://www.smkp.de/ueber-uns/geschichte/geschichte-architektur/ (abgerufen am 28.10.2016).

**25** Prof. Dr. Karin von Welck, Deutsche UNESCO-Kommission, am 18.10.2016 auf https://www.unesco.de/kultur/2016/unesco-weltbericht-kultur-urbane-zukunft.html. Die diesjährige Weltkonferenz für Siedlungs- und Stadtentwicklung *Habitat III* (17.–20.10.2016, Quito, Ecuador) stellt ein zentrales Instrument zur Umsetzung der Agenda 2030 für nachhaltige Entwicklung dar.

# Mischa Kuball

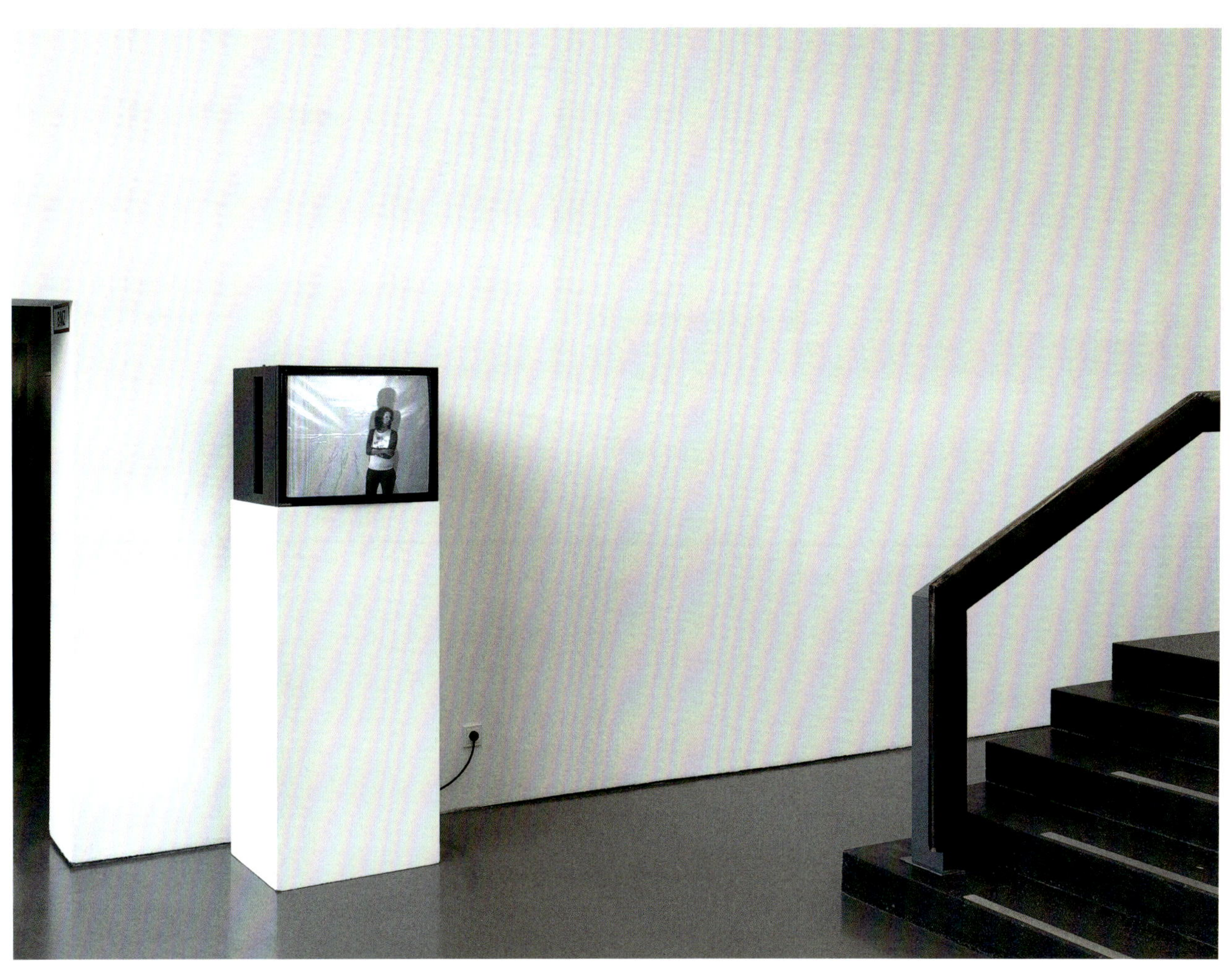

**Mischa Kuball**
‚platon's spiegel' Dokumentation 1, 2011

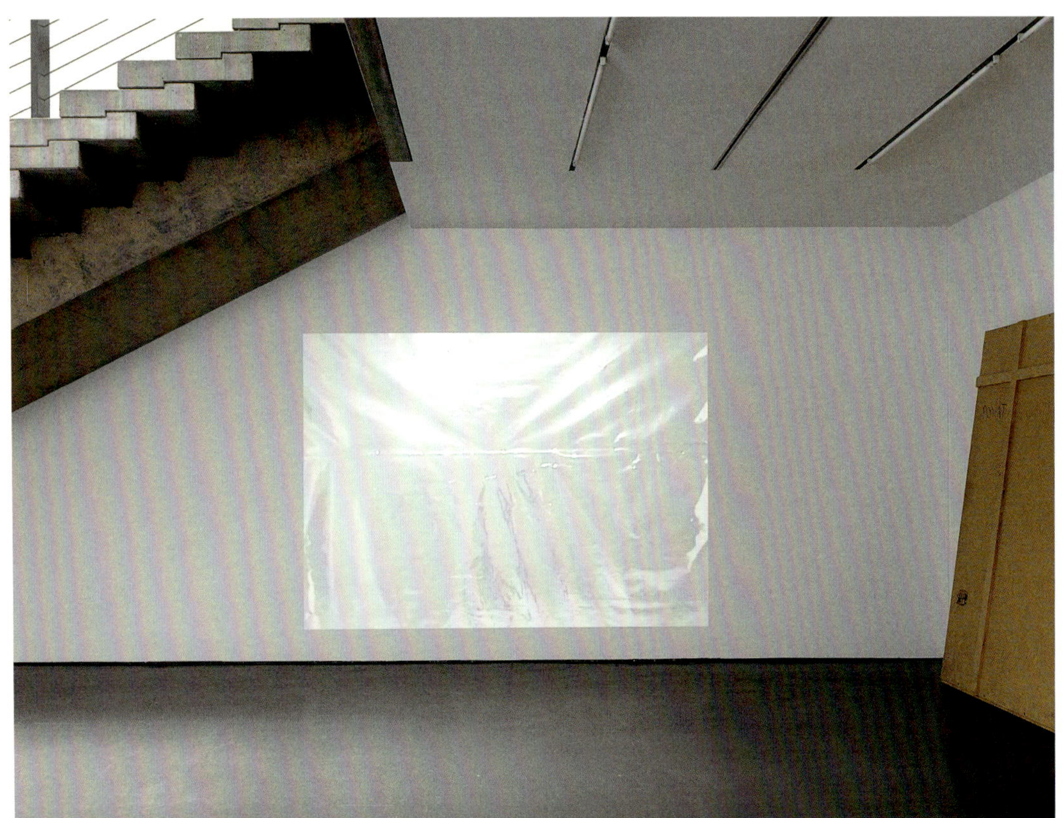

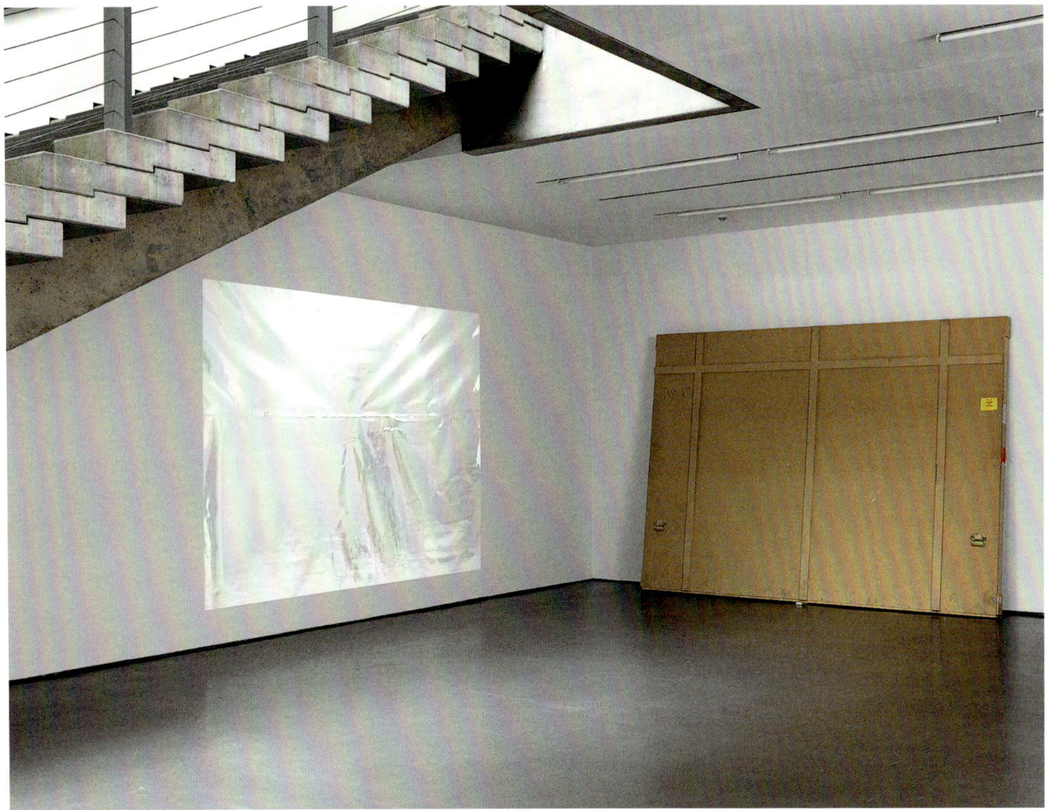

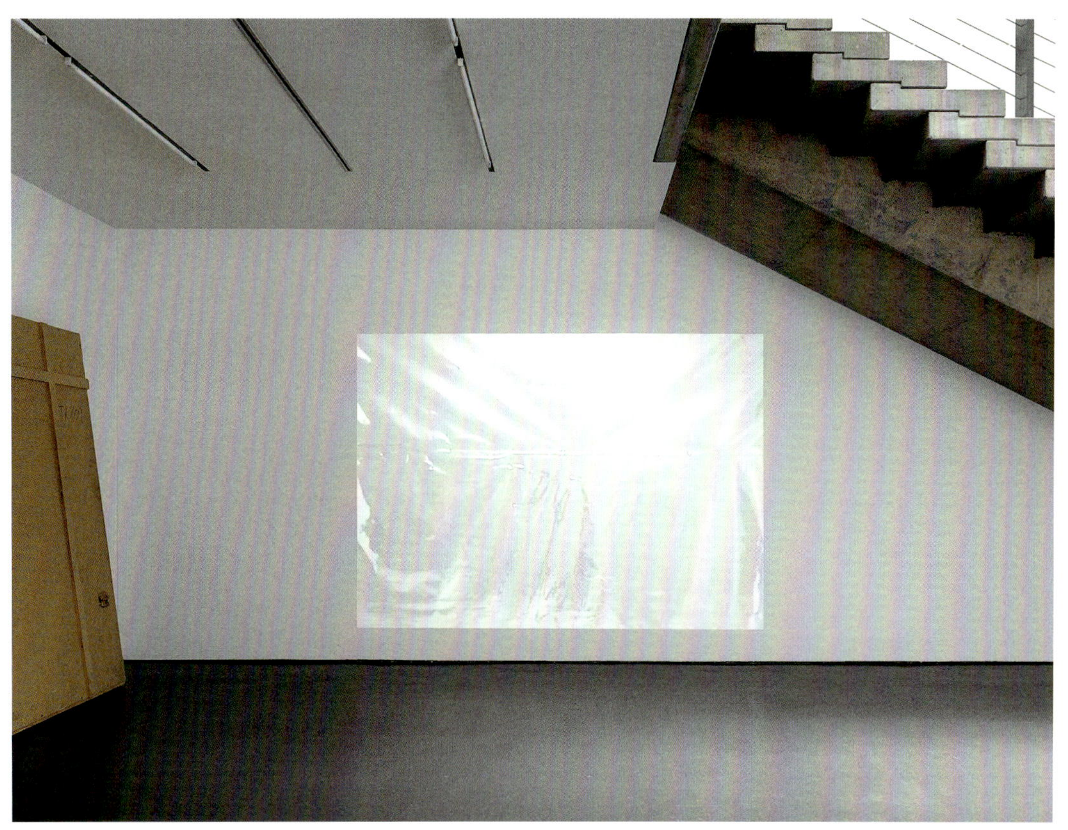

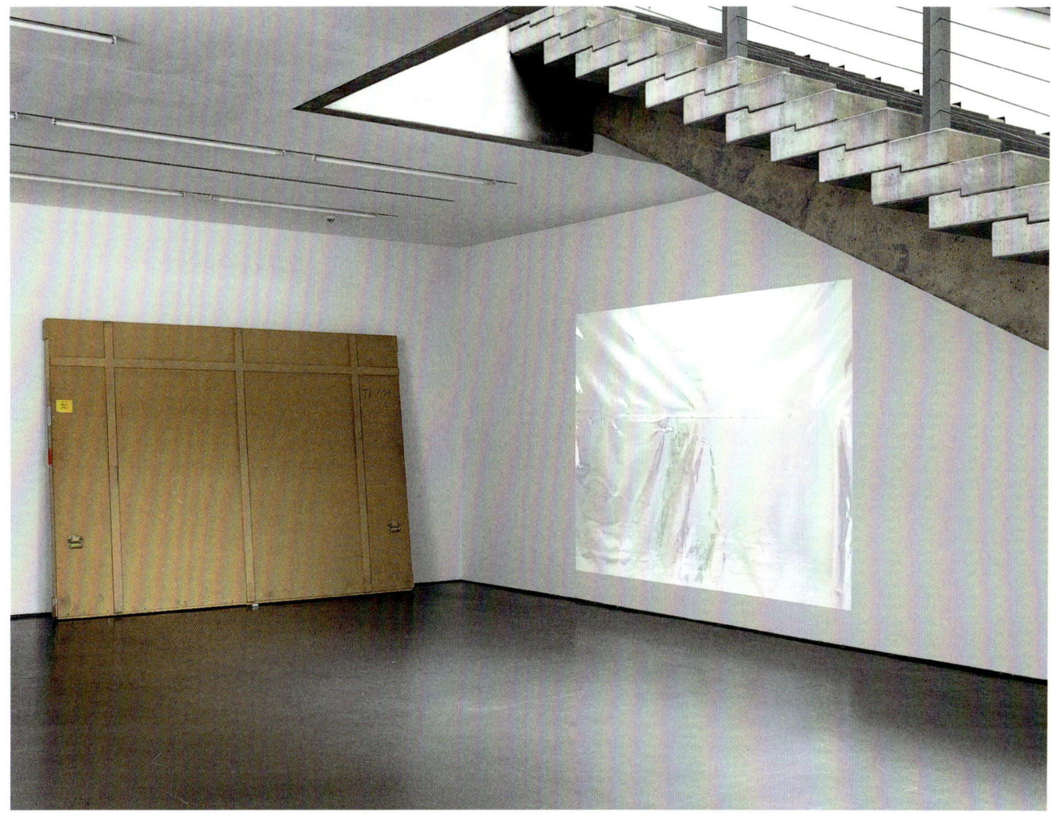

**Mischa Kuball**
‚platon's spiegel', 2009

# Gerhard Richter

# Gerhard Richter

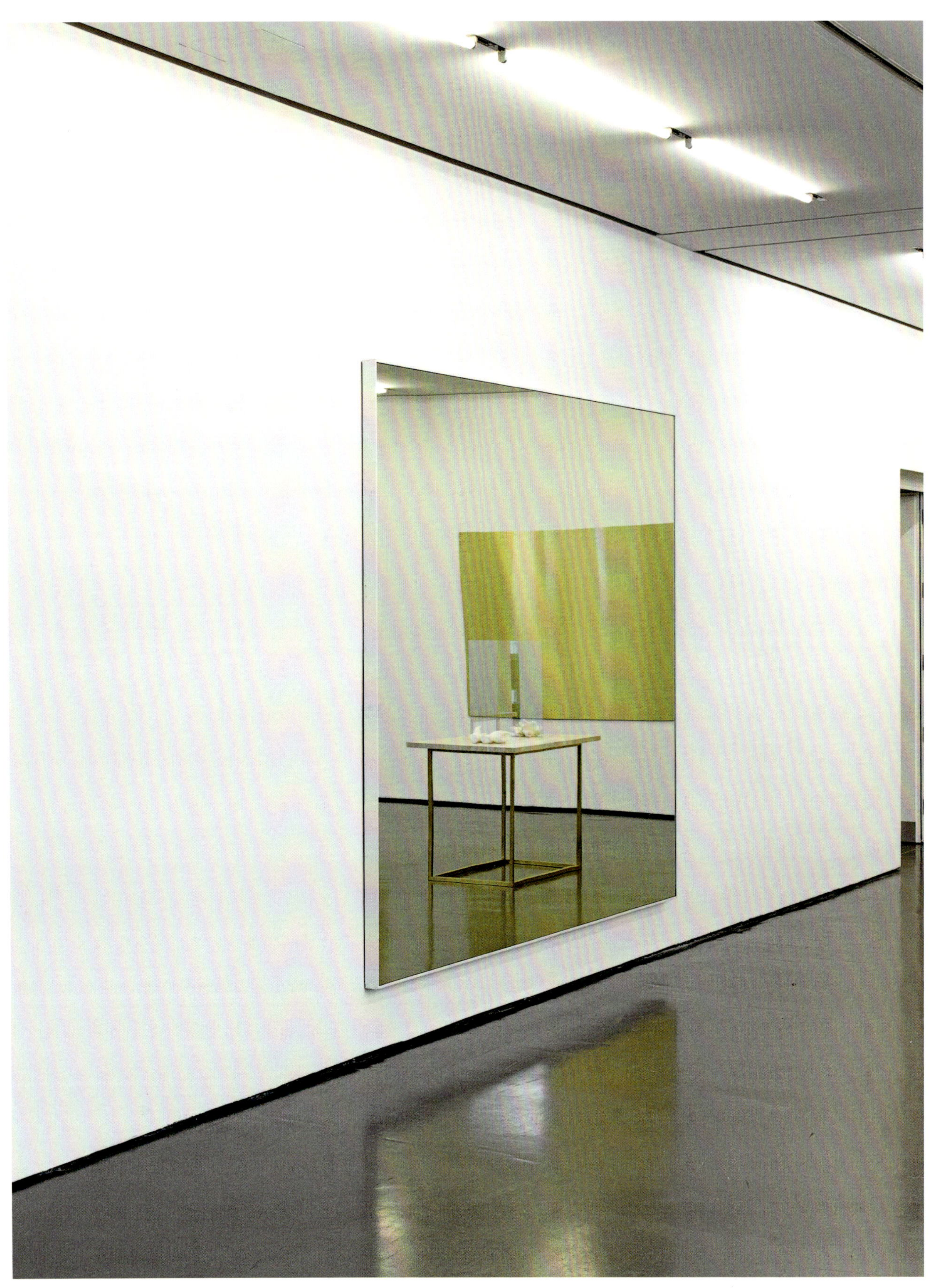

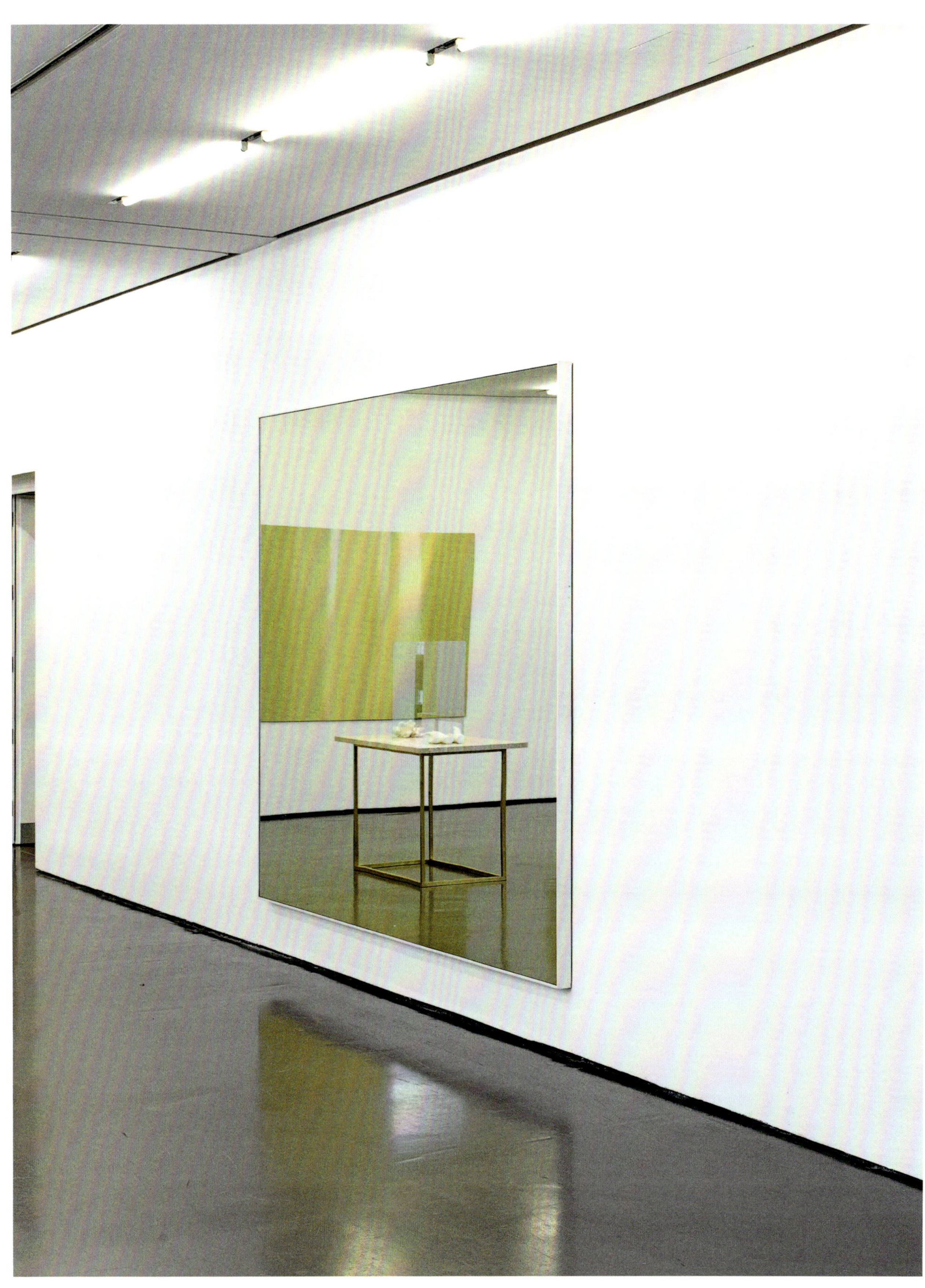

**Gerhard Richter**
Spiegel, 1981

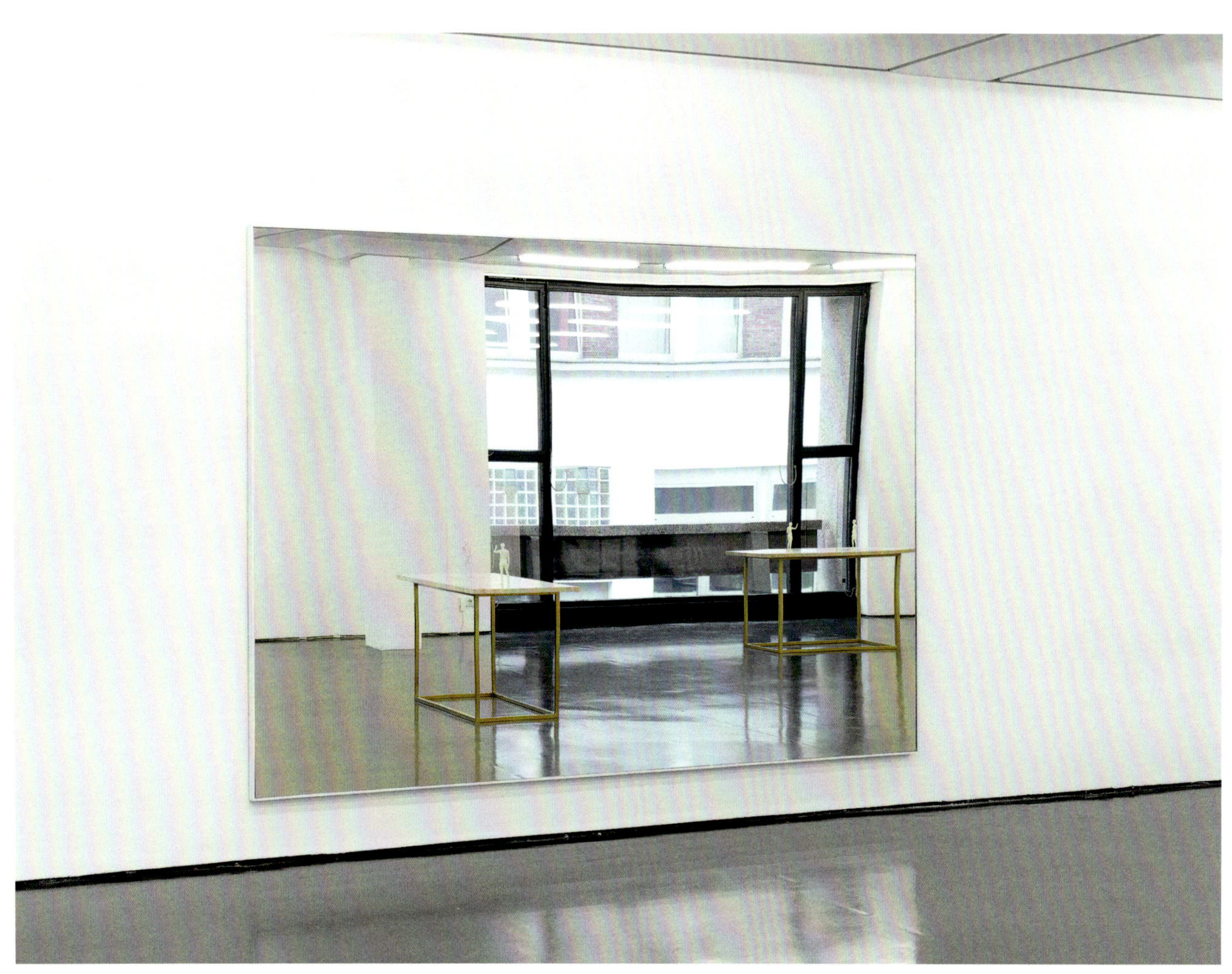

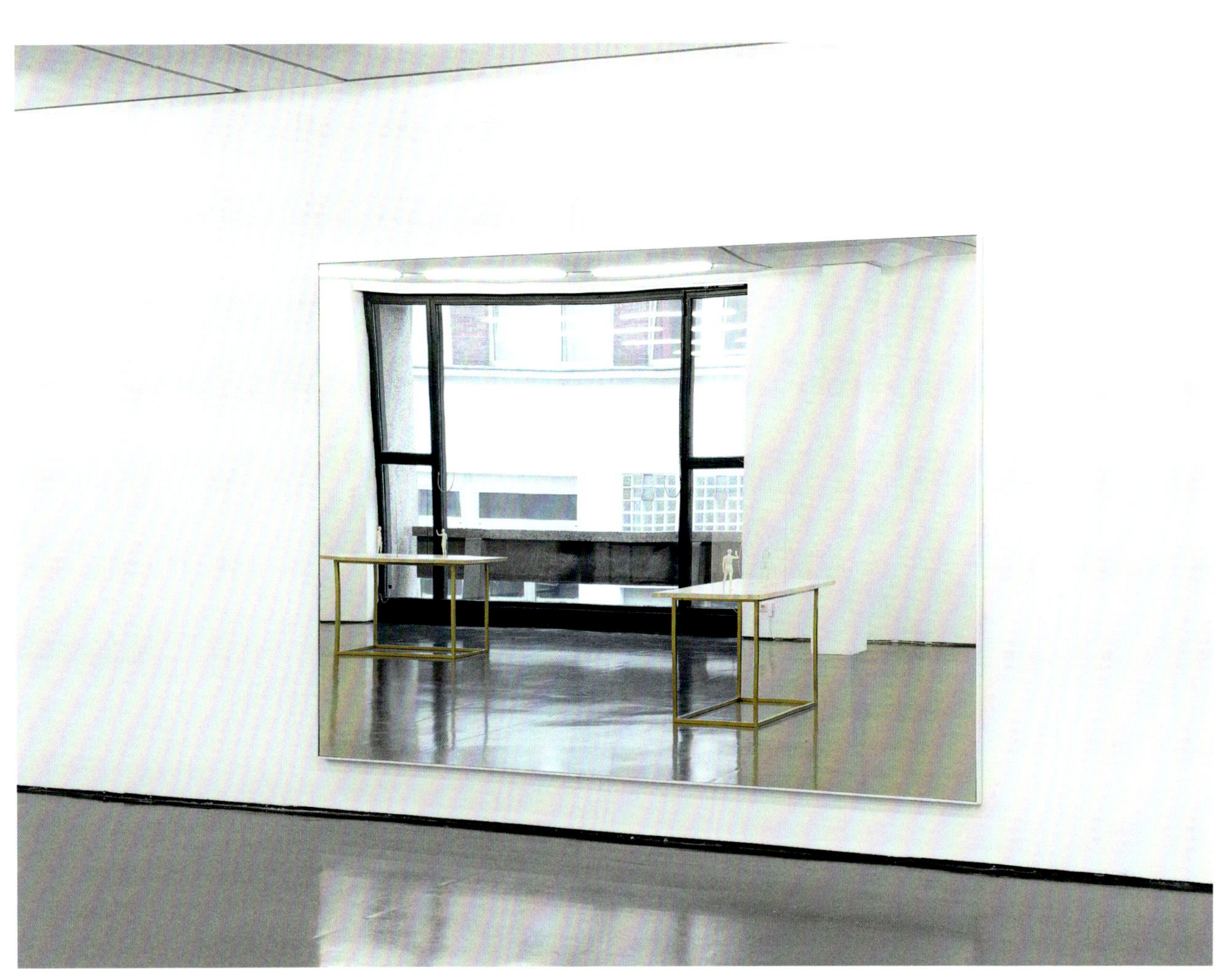

**Gerhard Richter**
Spiegel, 1981

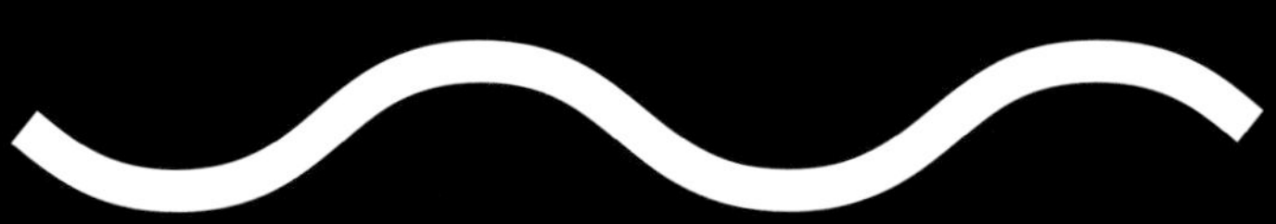

# Aron Mehzion

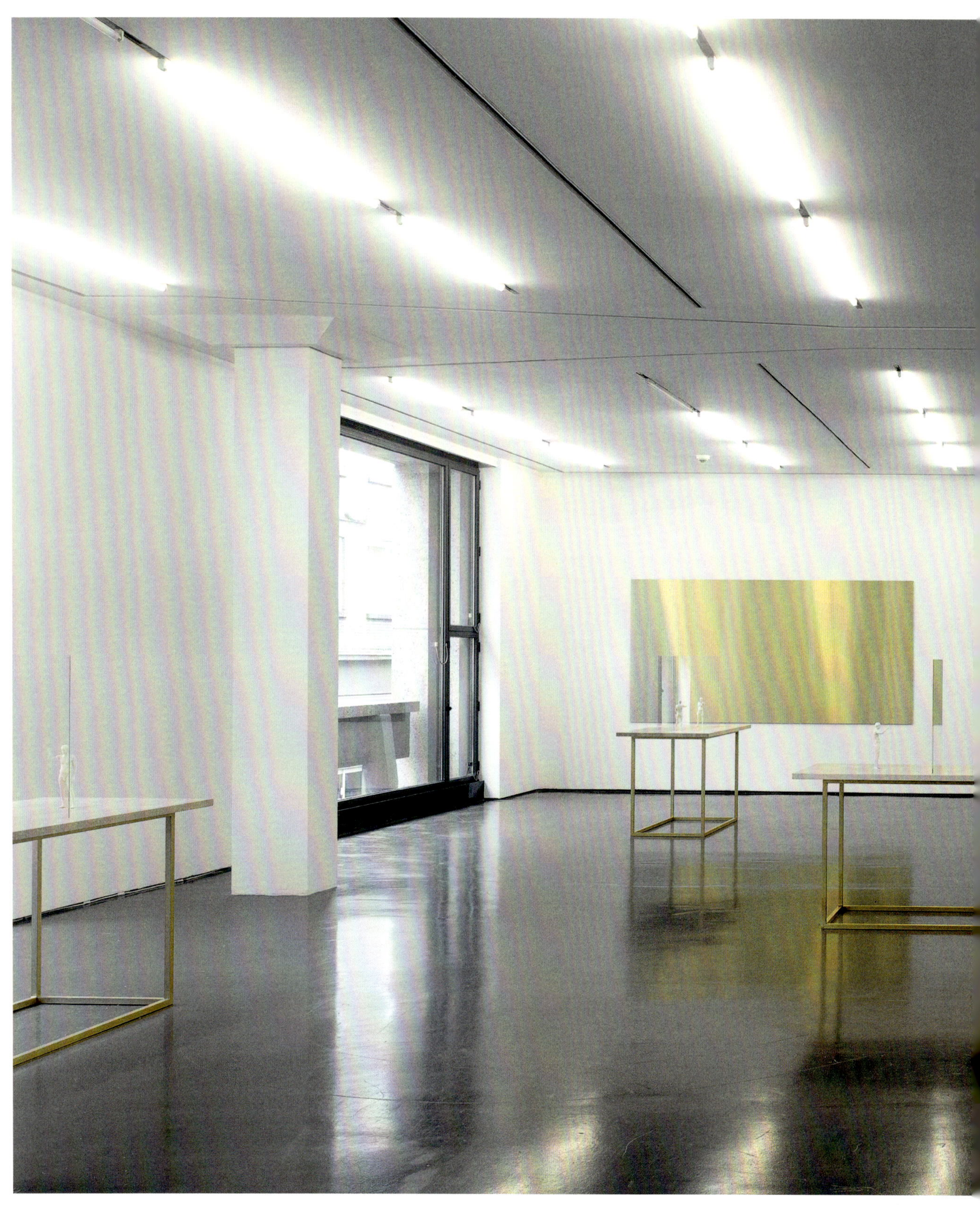

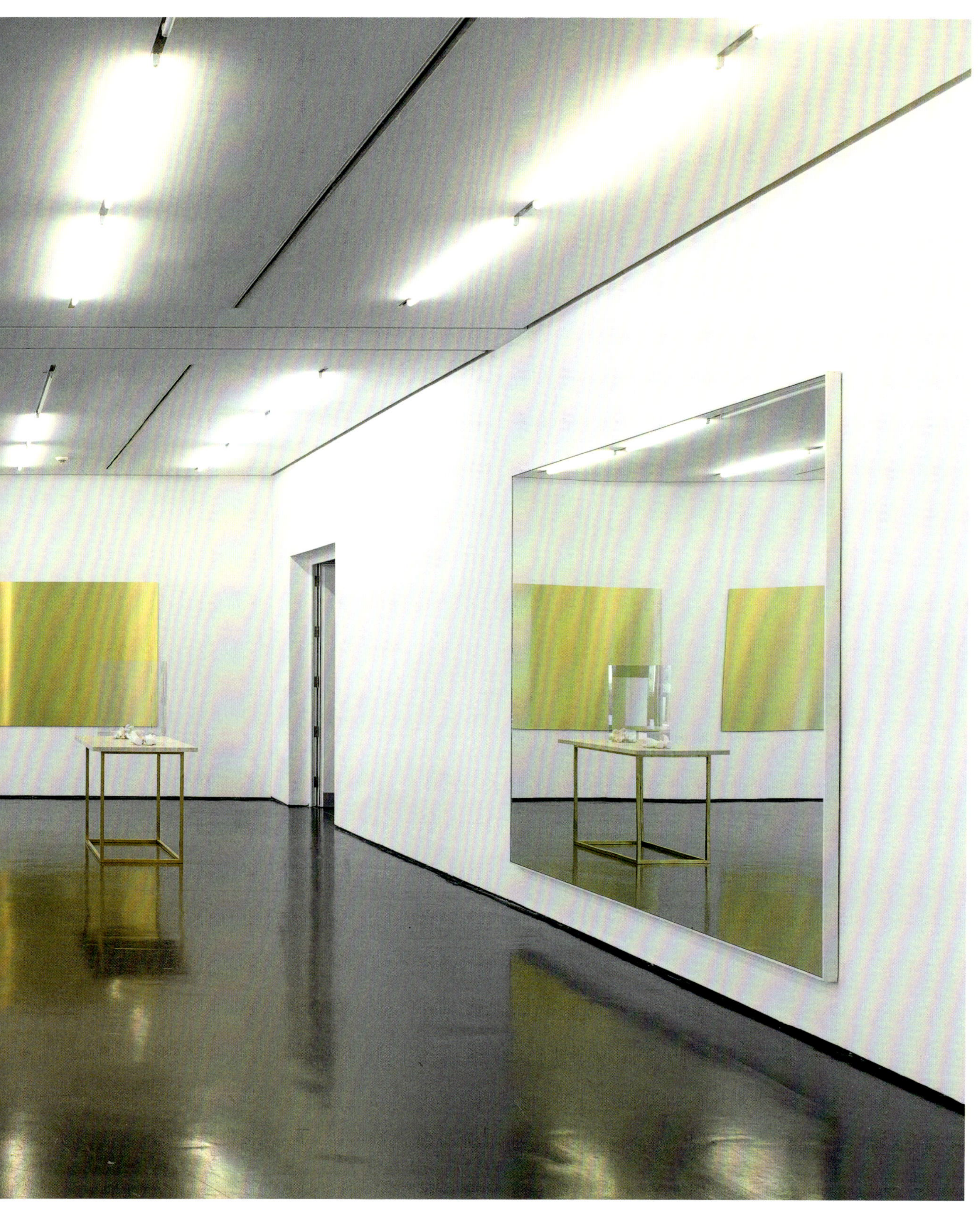

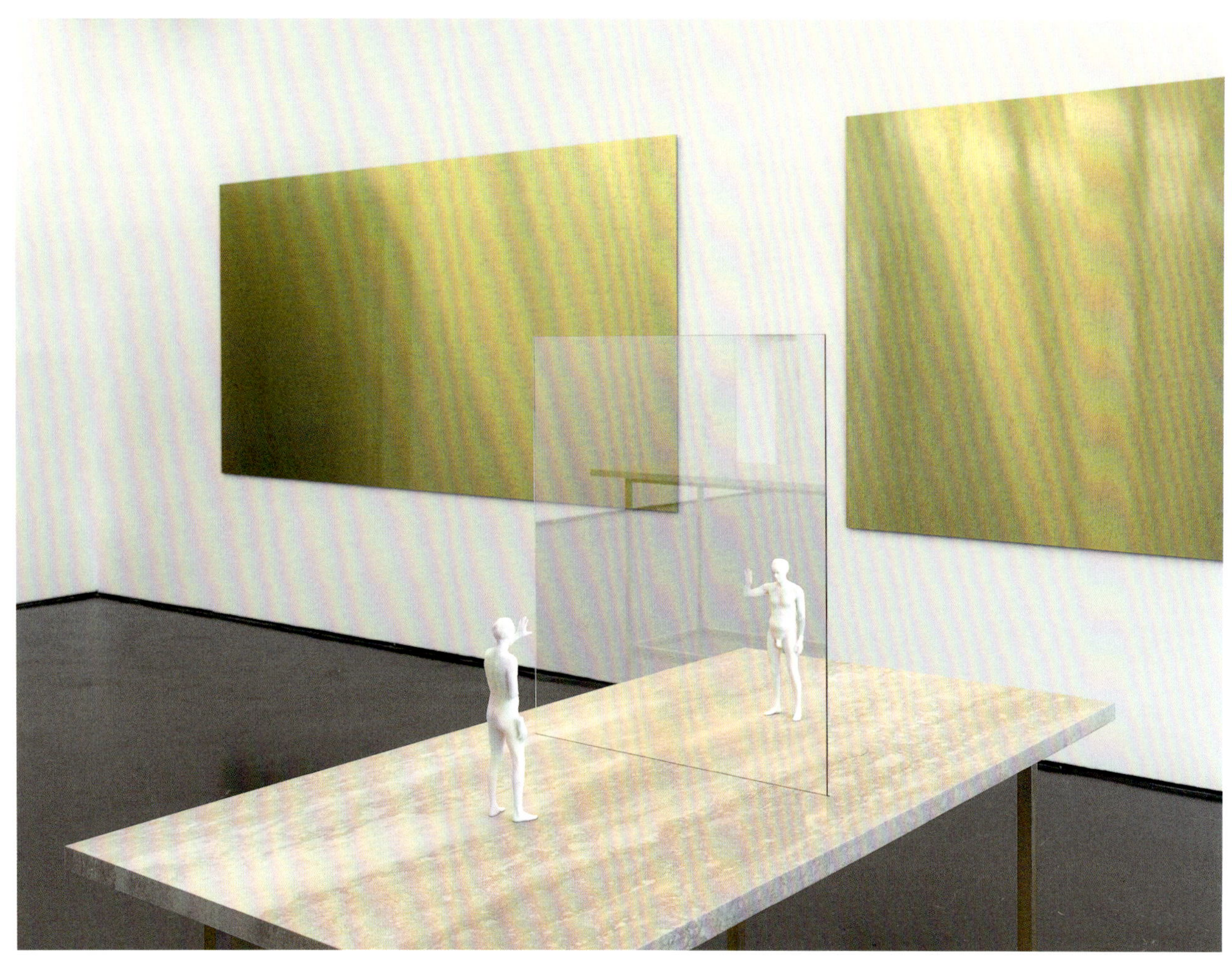

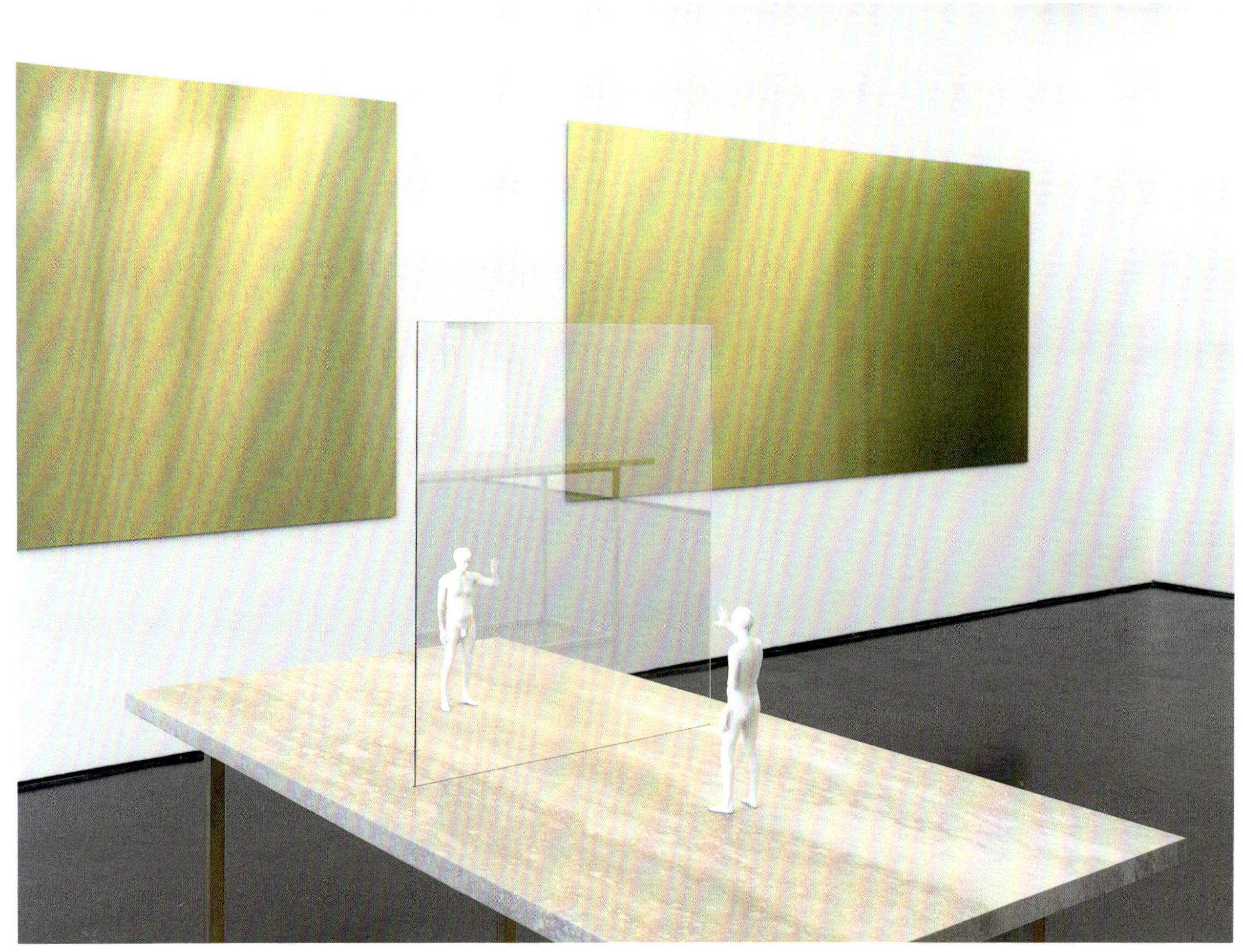

**Aron Mehzion**
A' I A', 2016

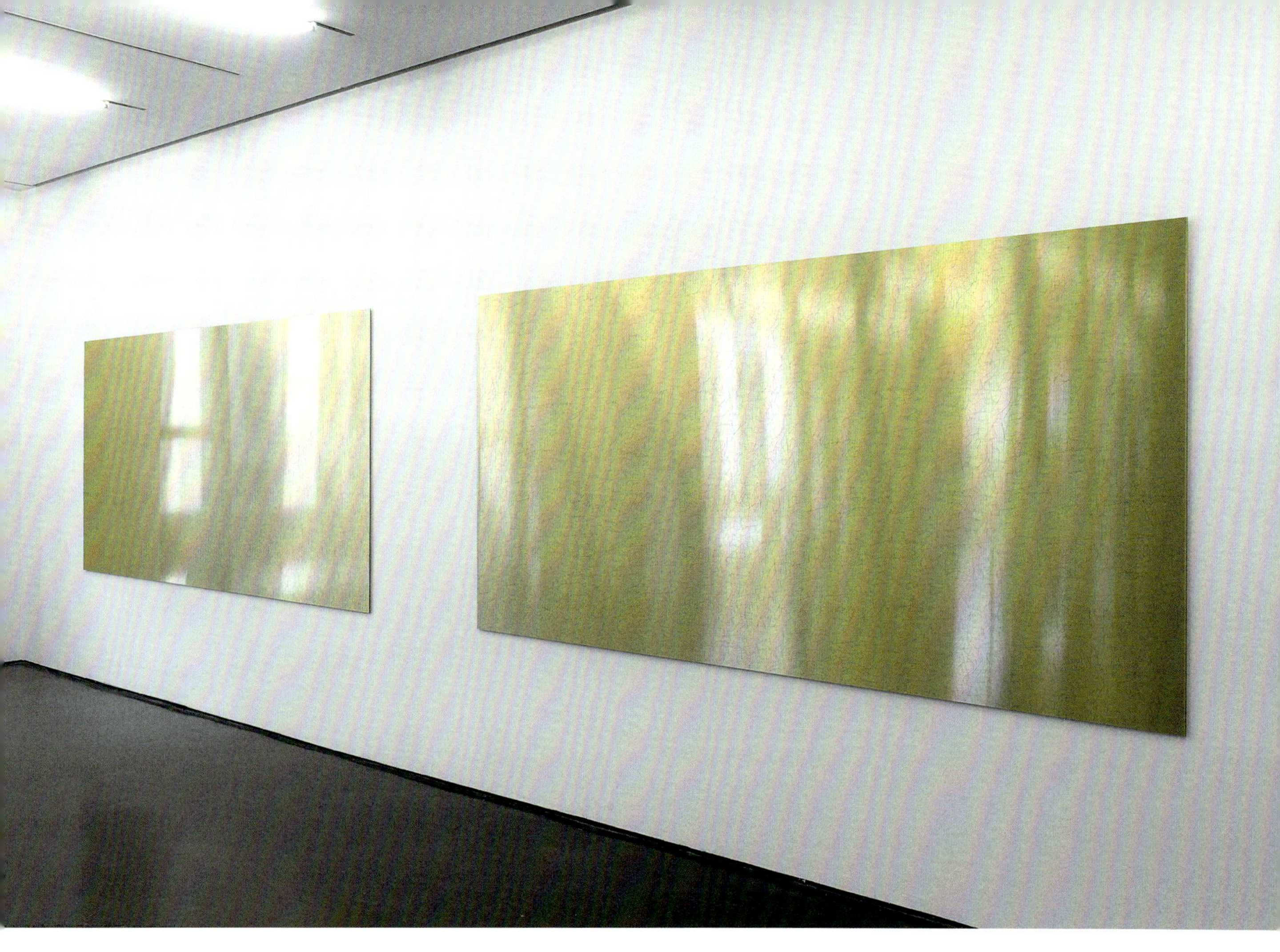

**Aron Mehzion**
Passage VII und VIII, 2016

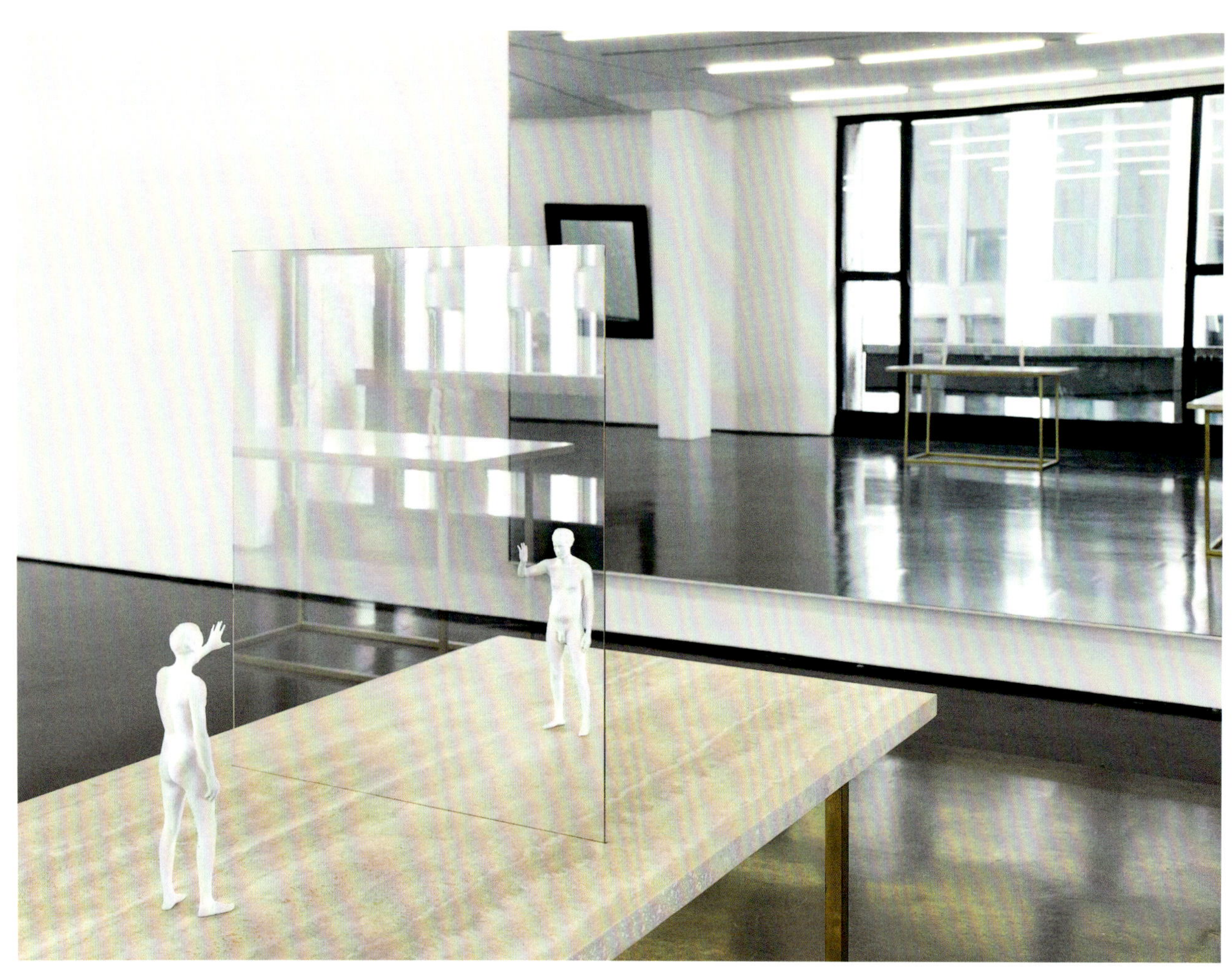

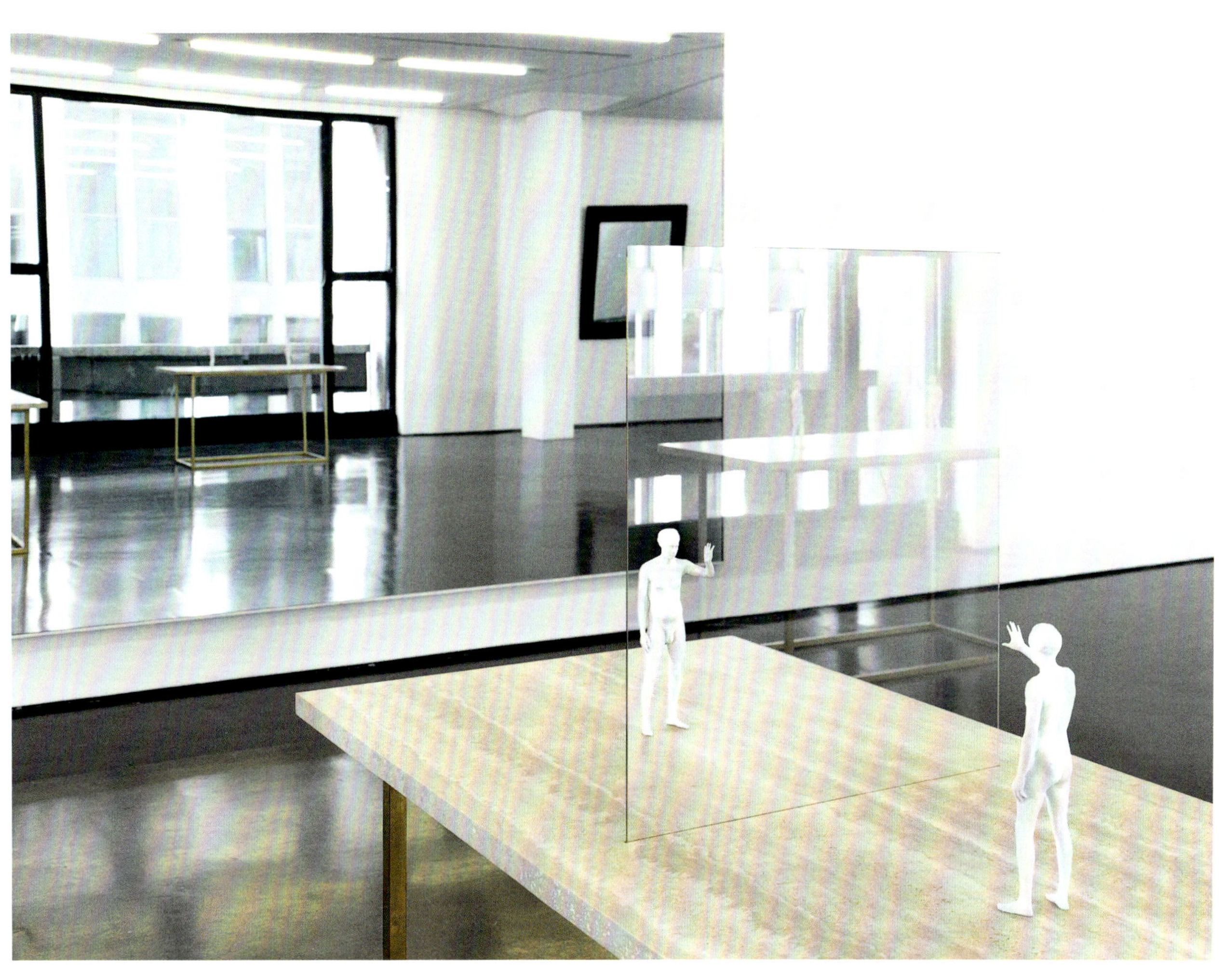

**Aron Mehzion**
A I A, 2016

# Lili Dujourie

# Lili Dujourie

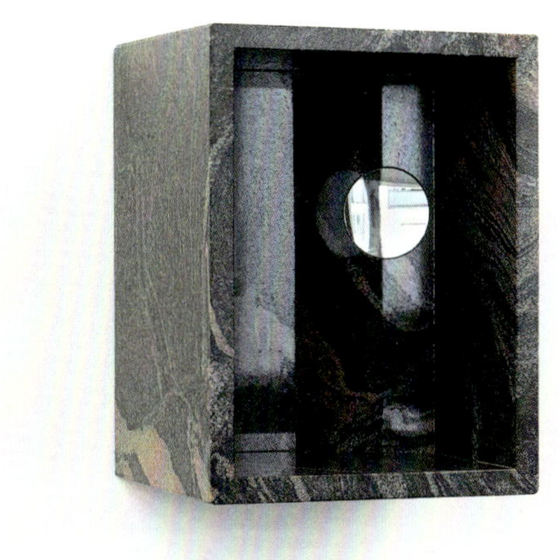

**Lili Dujourie**
Portret, 1987

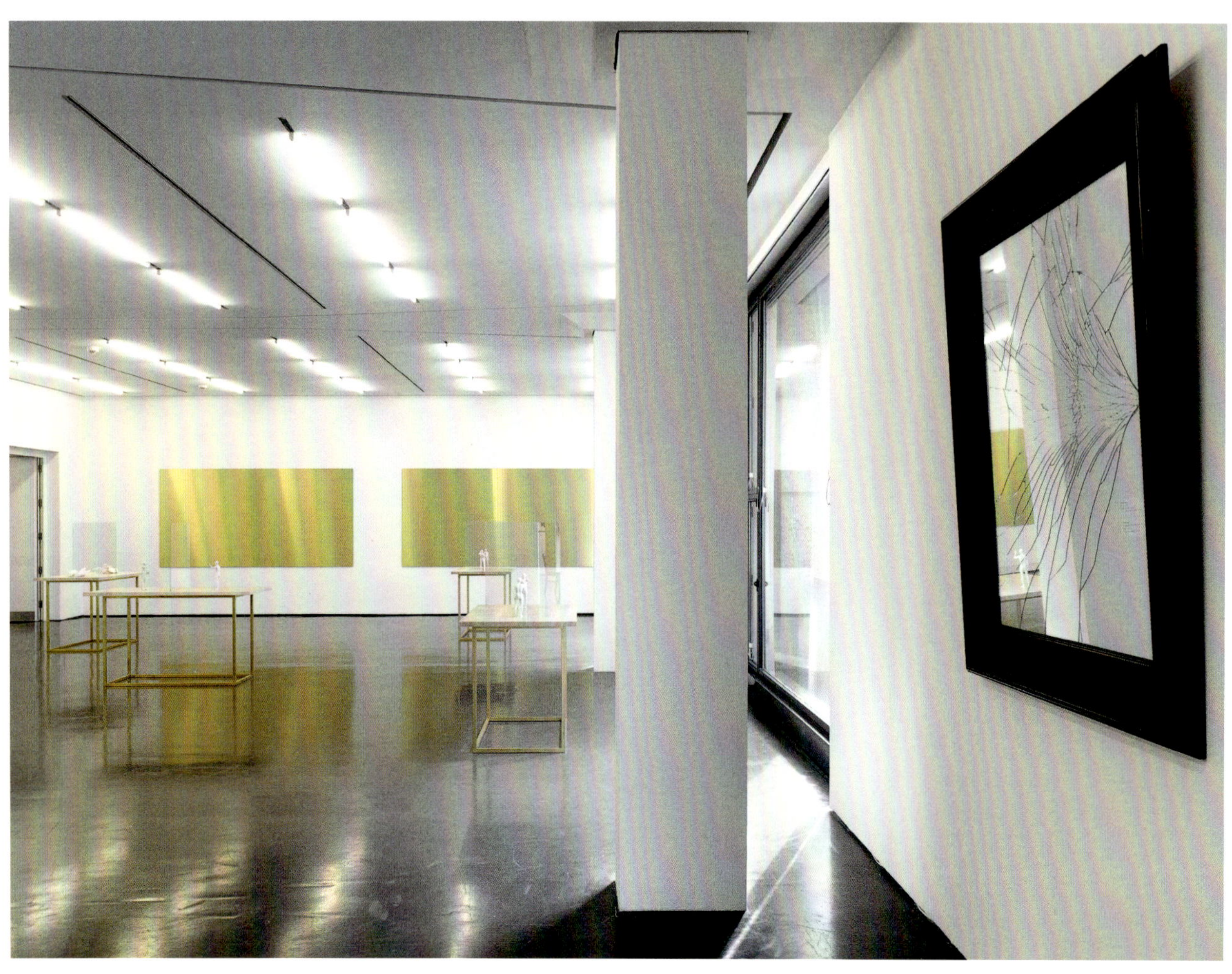

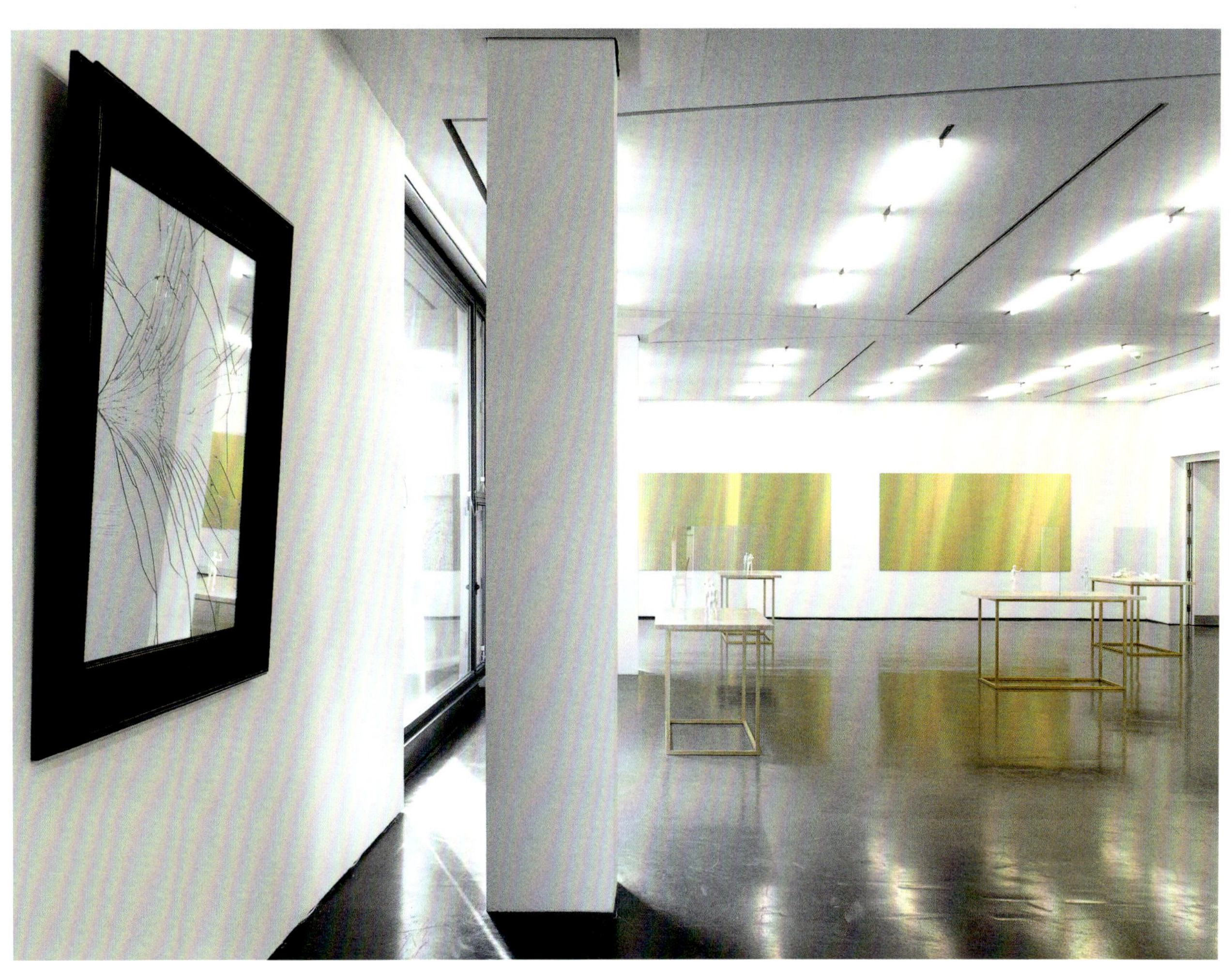

**Lili Dujourie**
Portret, 1985

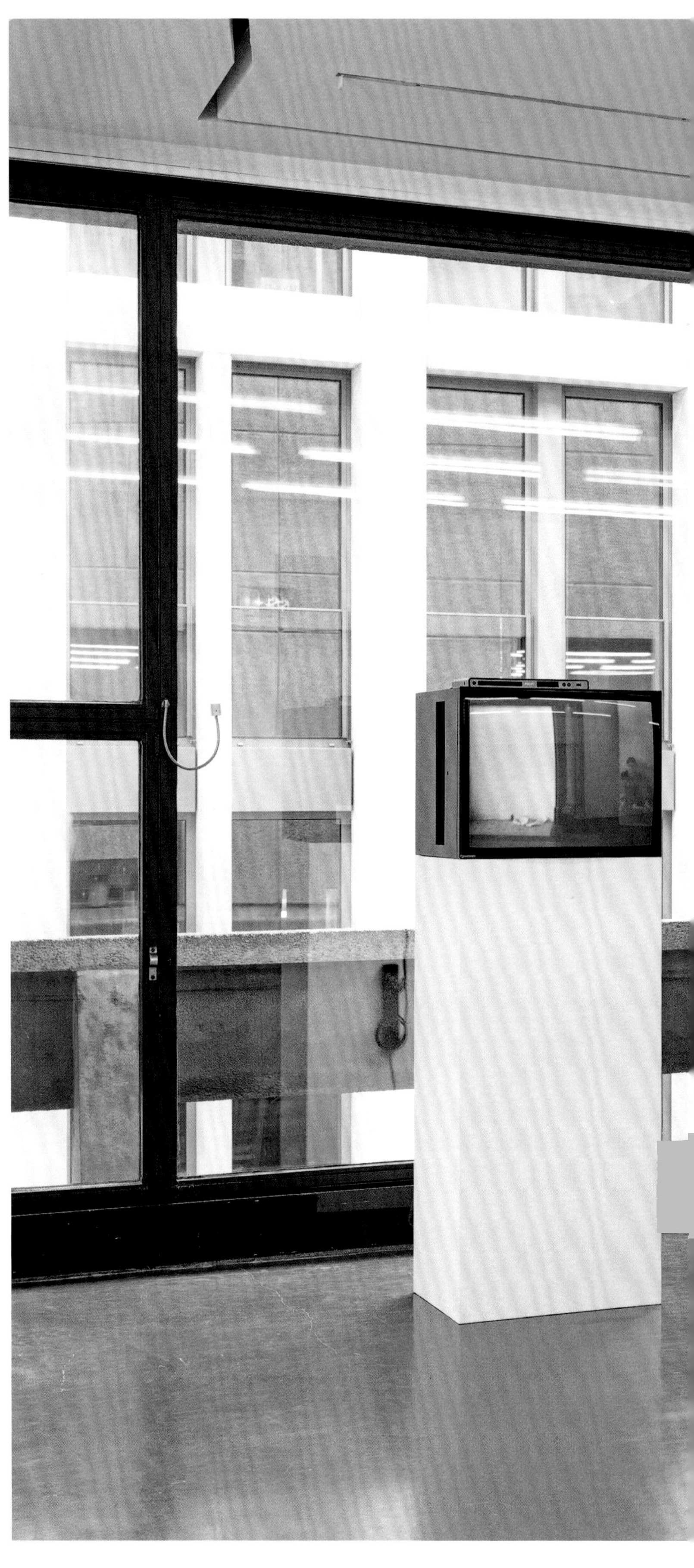

**Lili Dujourie**
Effen Spiegel van een stille stroom, 1976

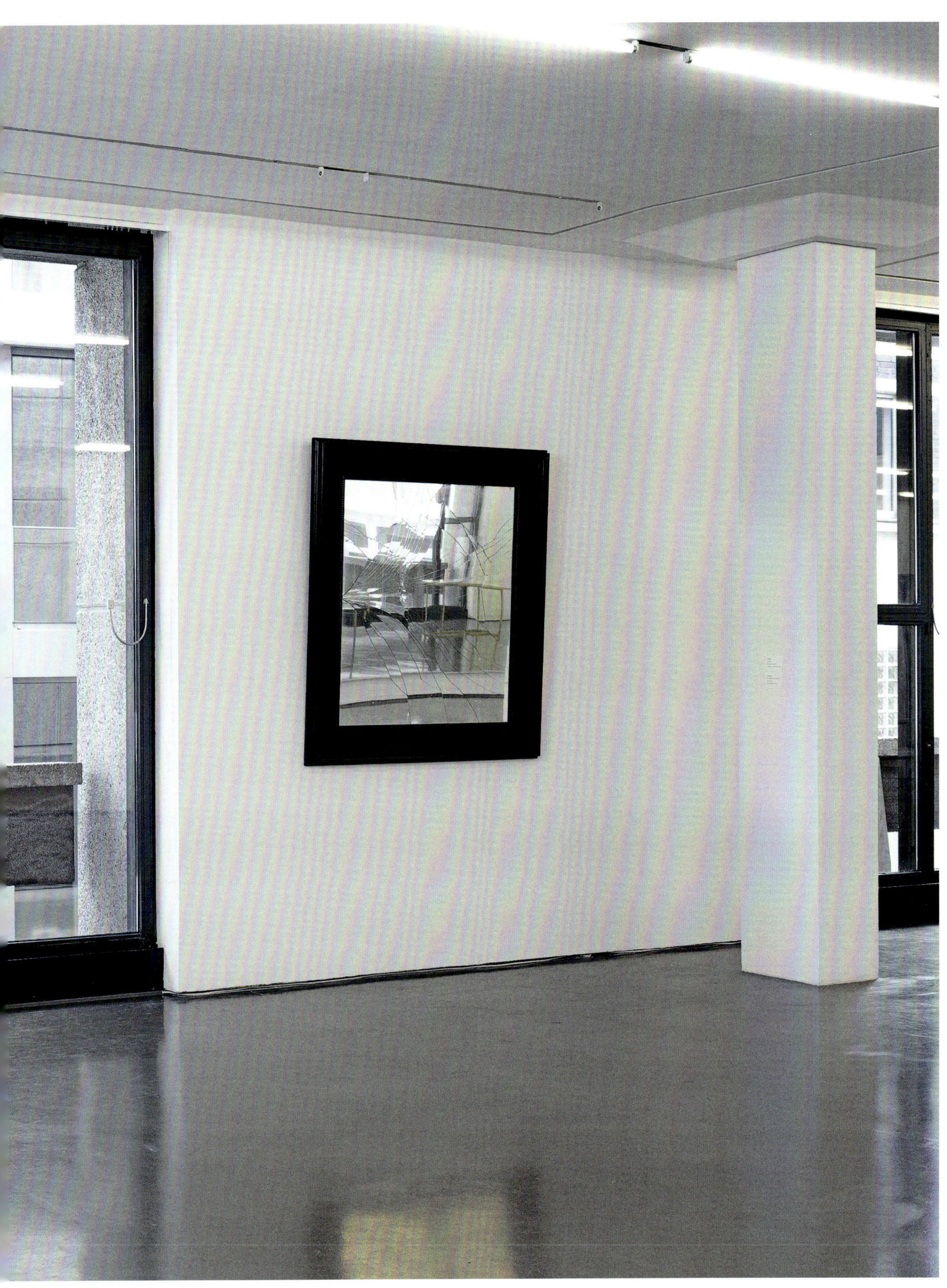

**Lili Dujourie**
Portret, 1985

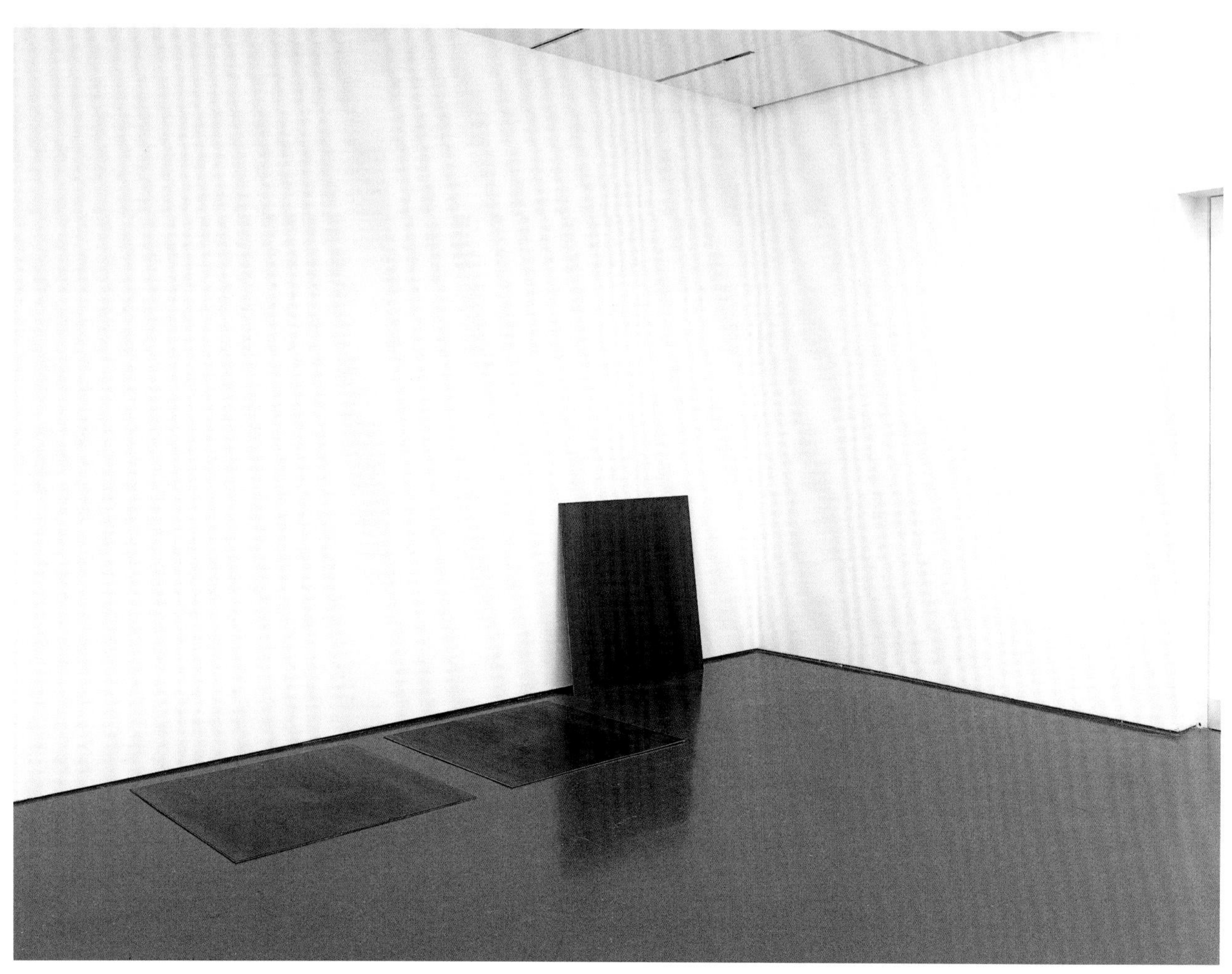

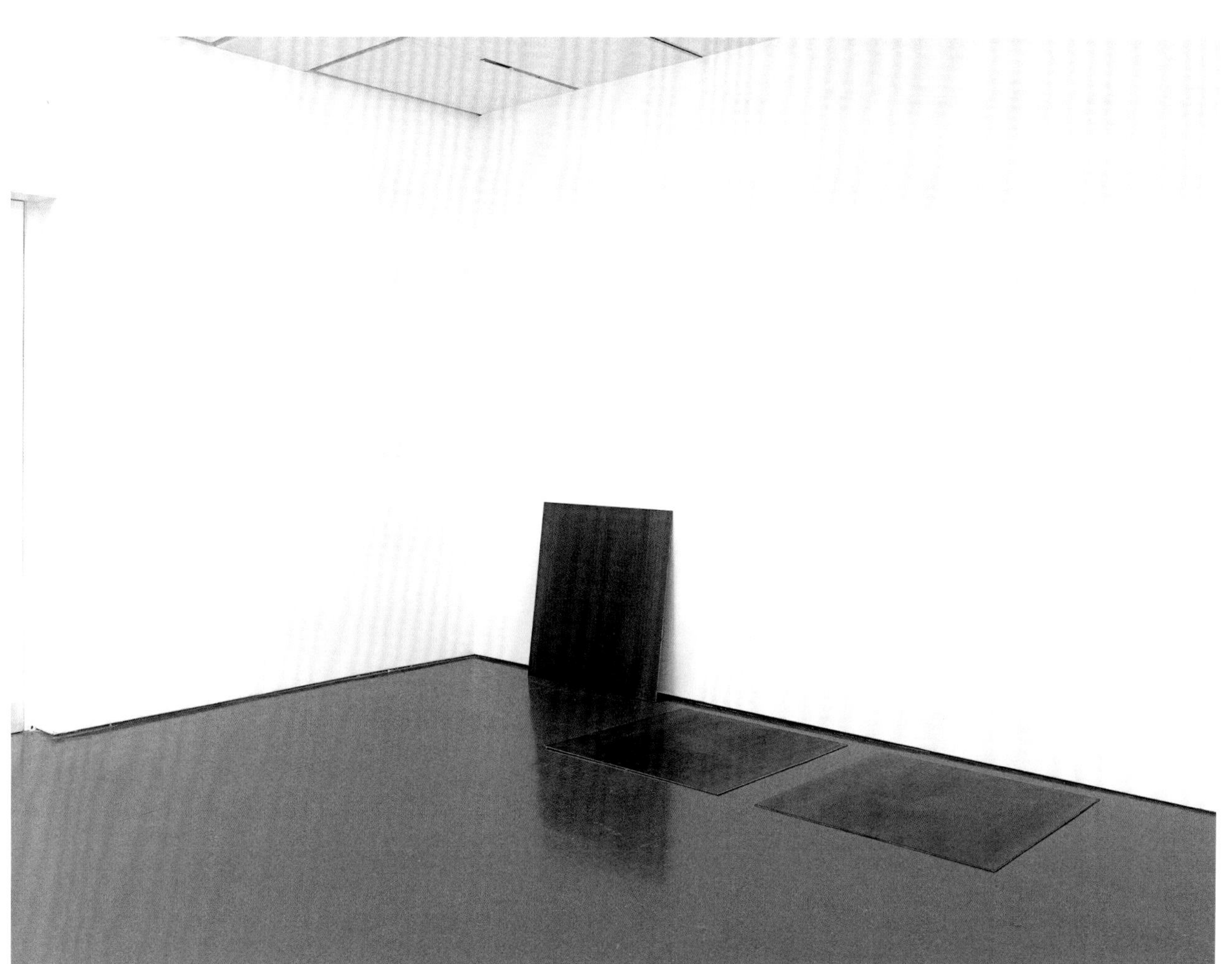

**Lili Dujourie**
Untitled, 1970

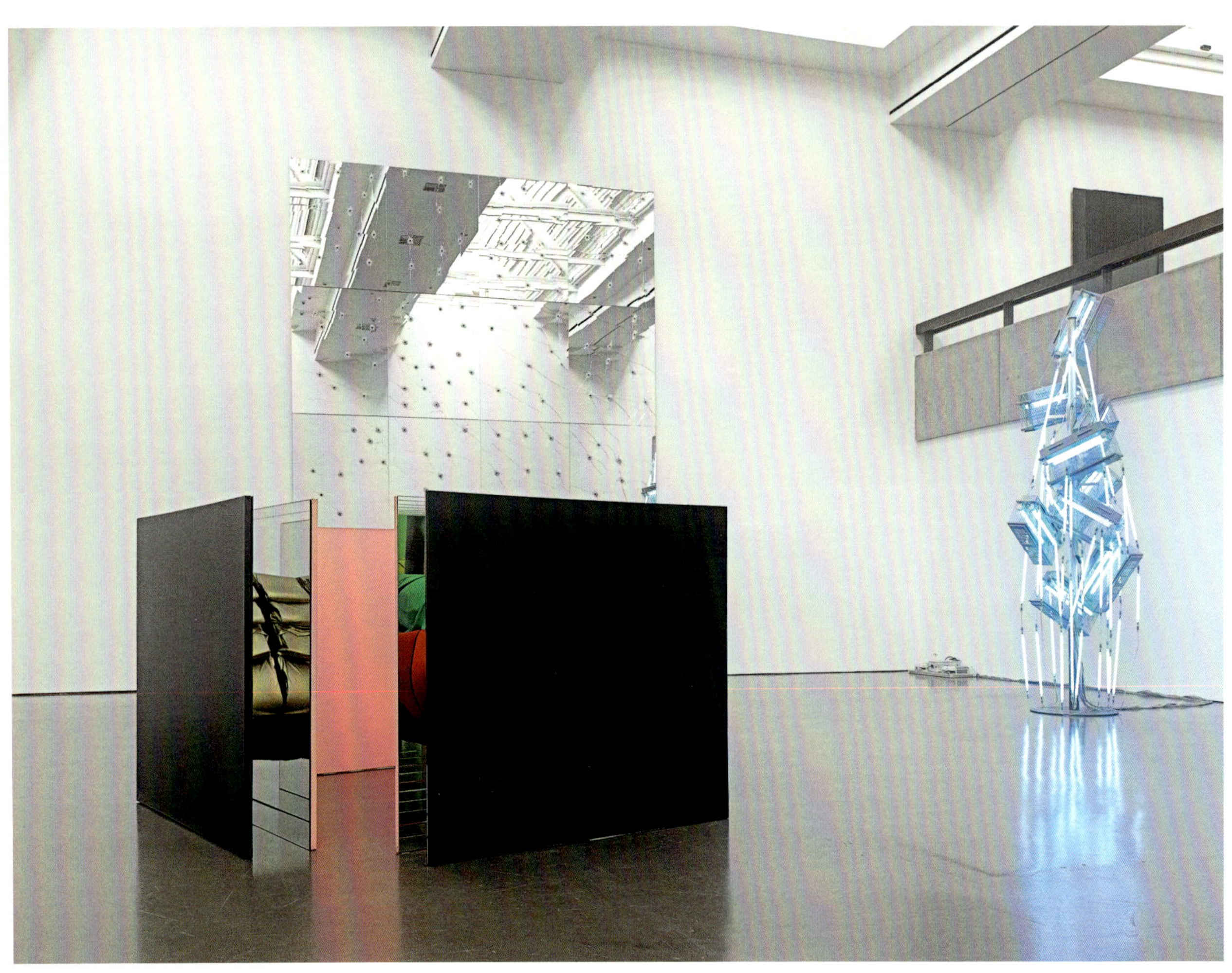

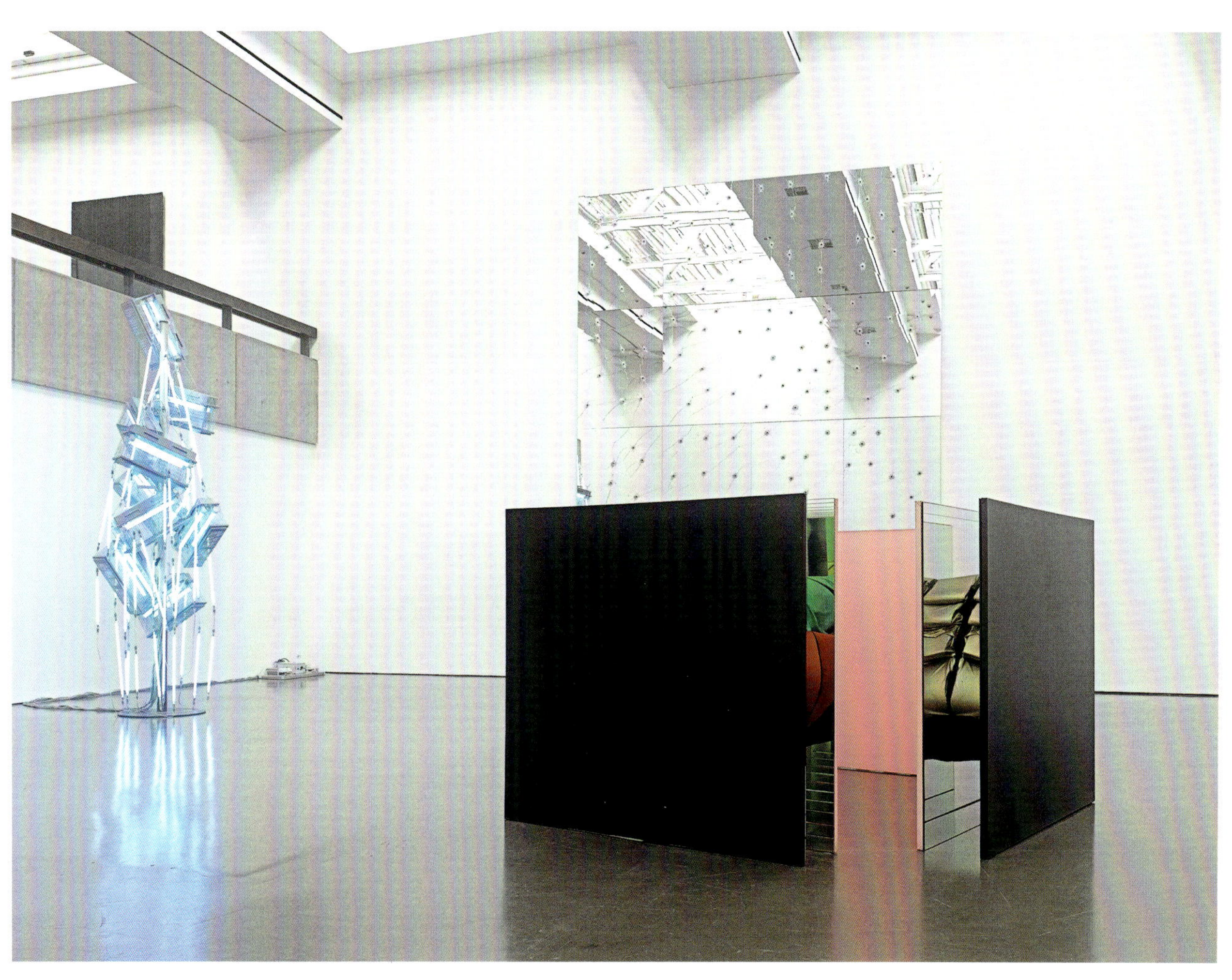

**Lili Dujourie**
Between Black and Pink, 1986

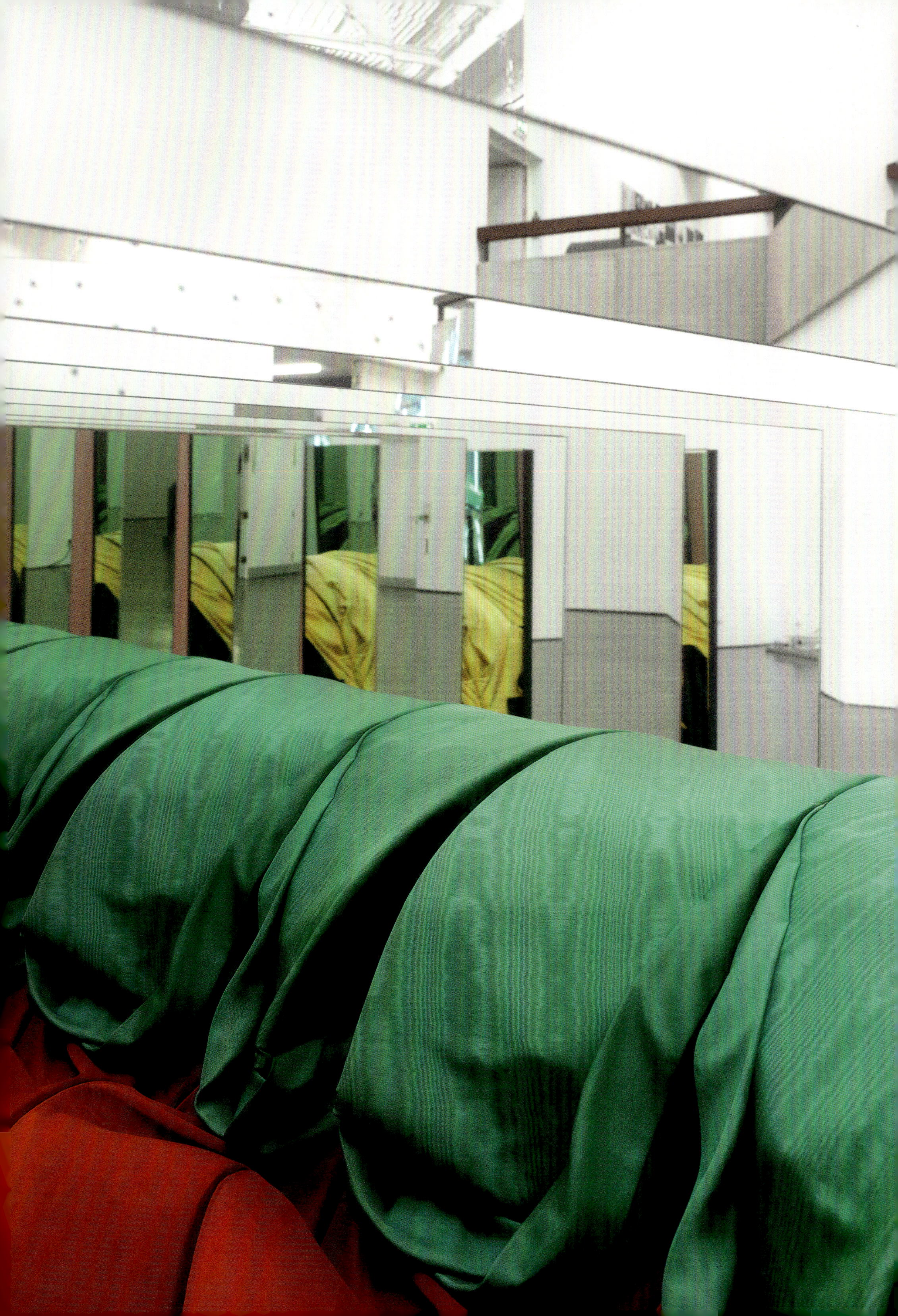

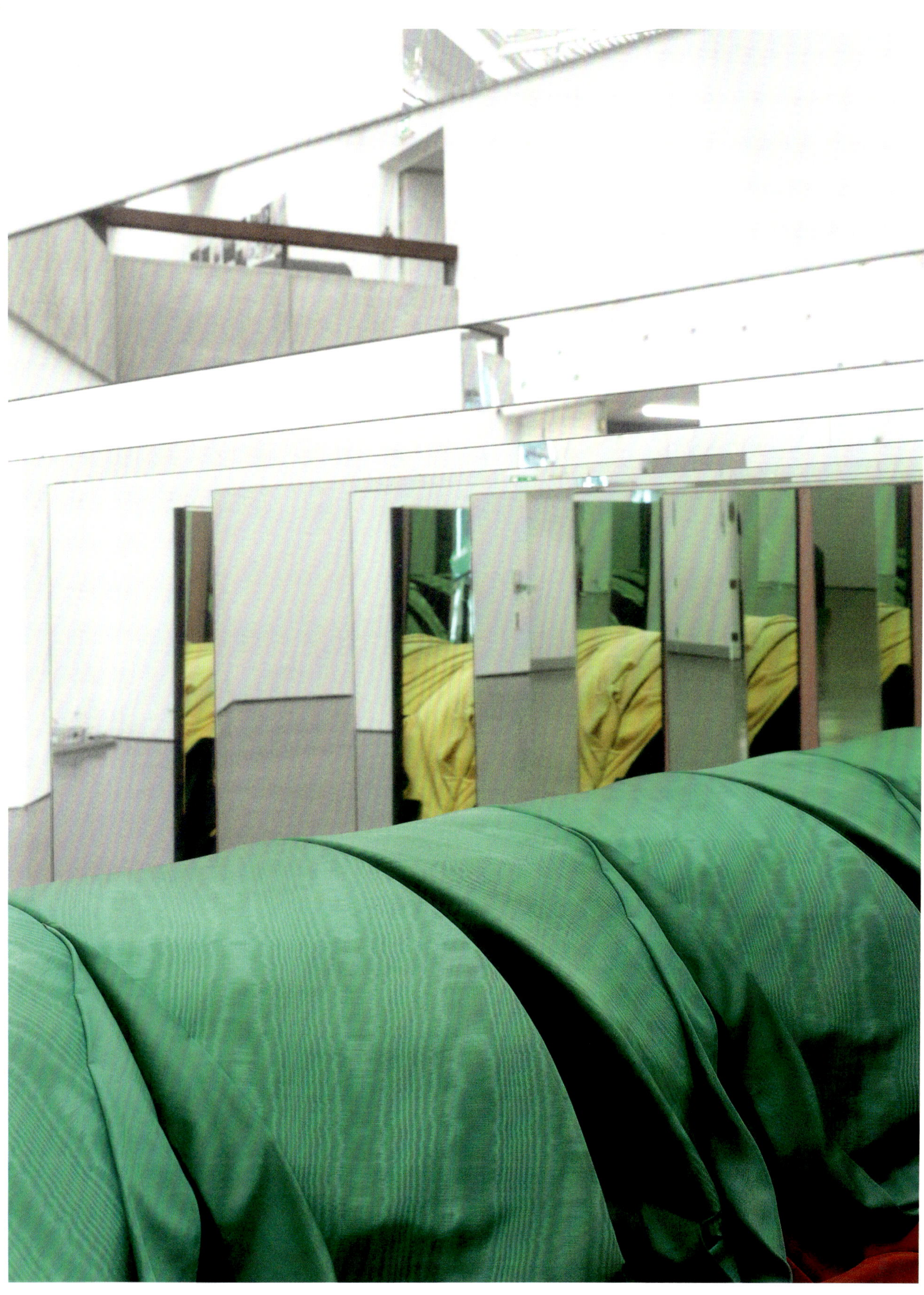

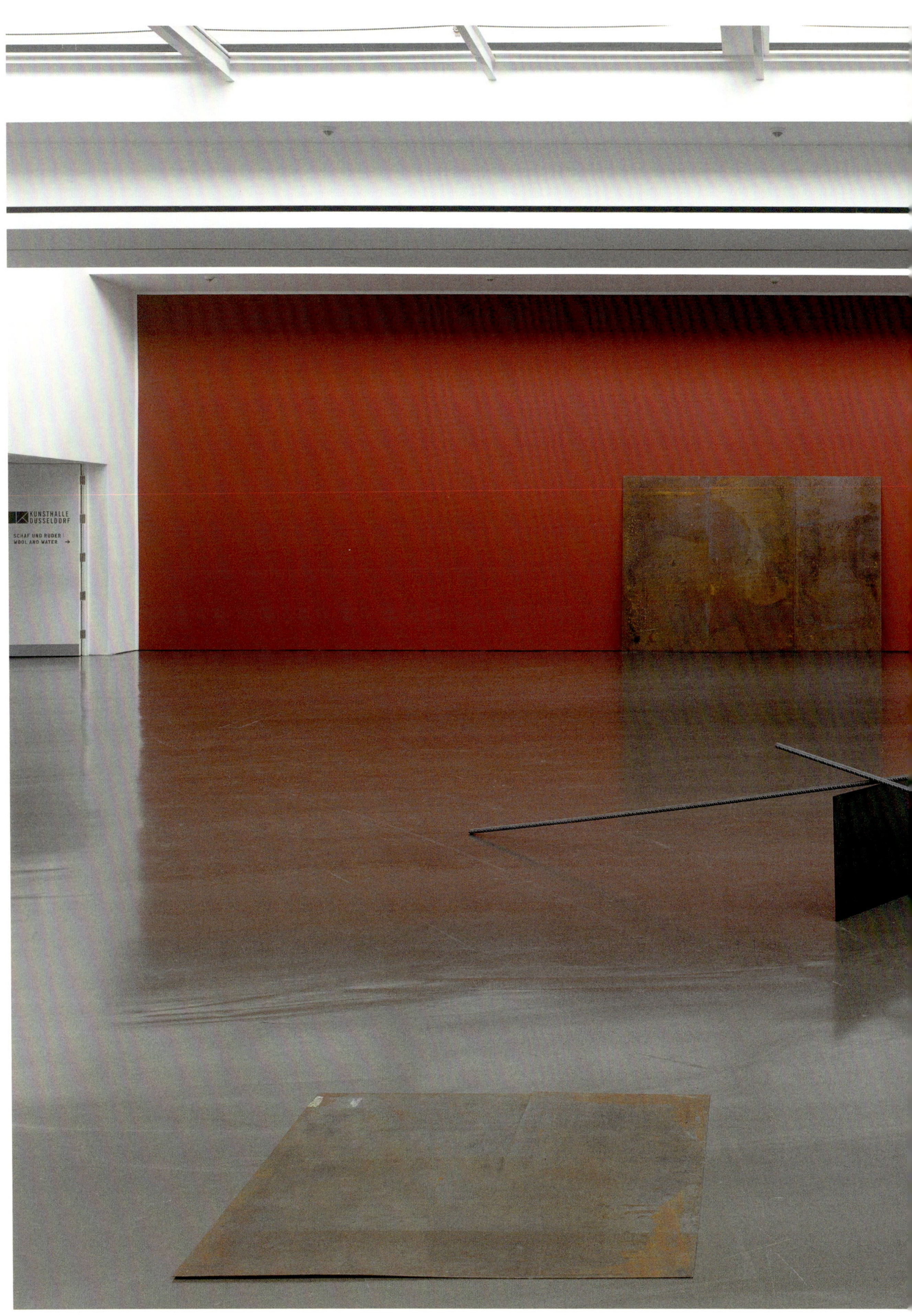
KUNSTHALLE
DUSSELDORF
SCHAF UND RUDER |
WOOL AND WATER →

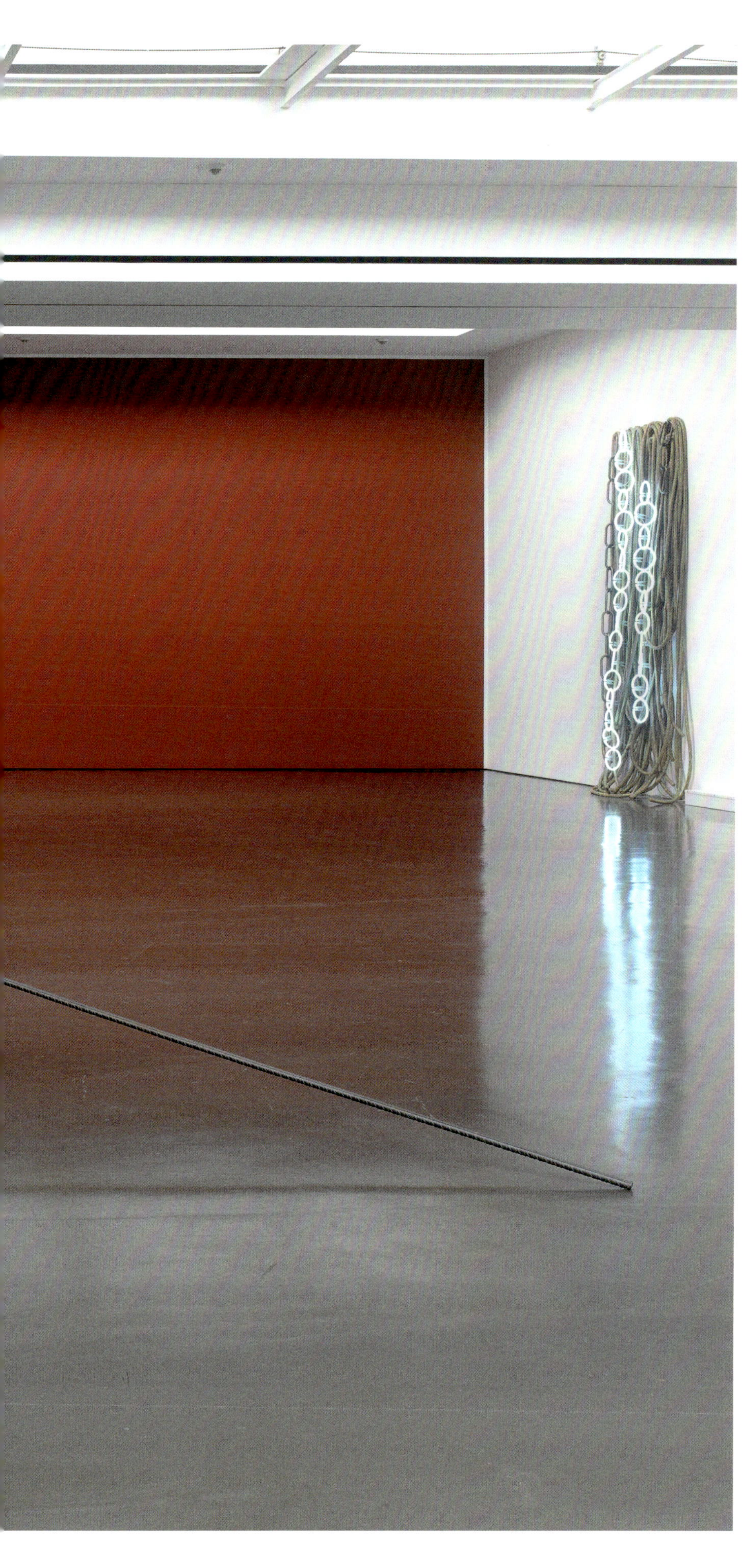

**Lili Dujourie**
Amerikaans Imperialism, 1972–2016

Untitled, 1967

Untitled, 1967

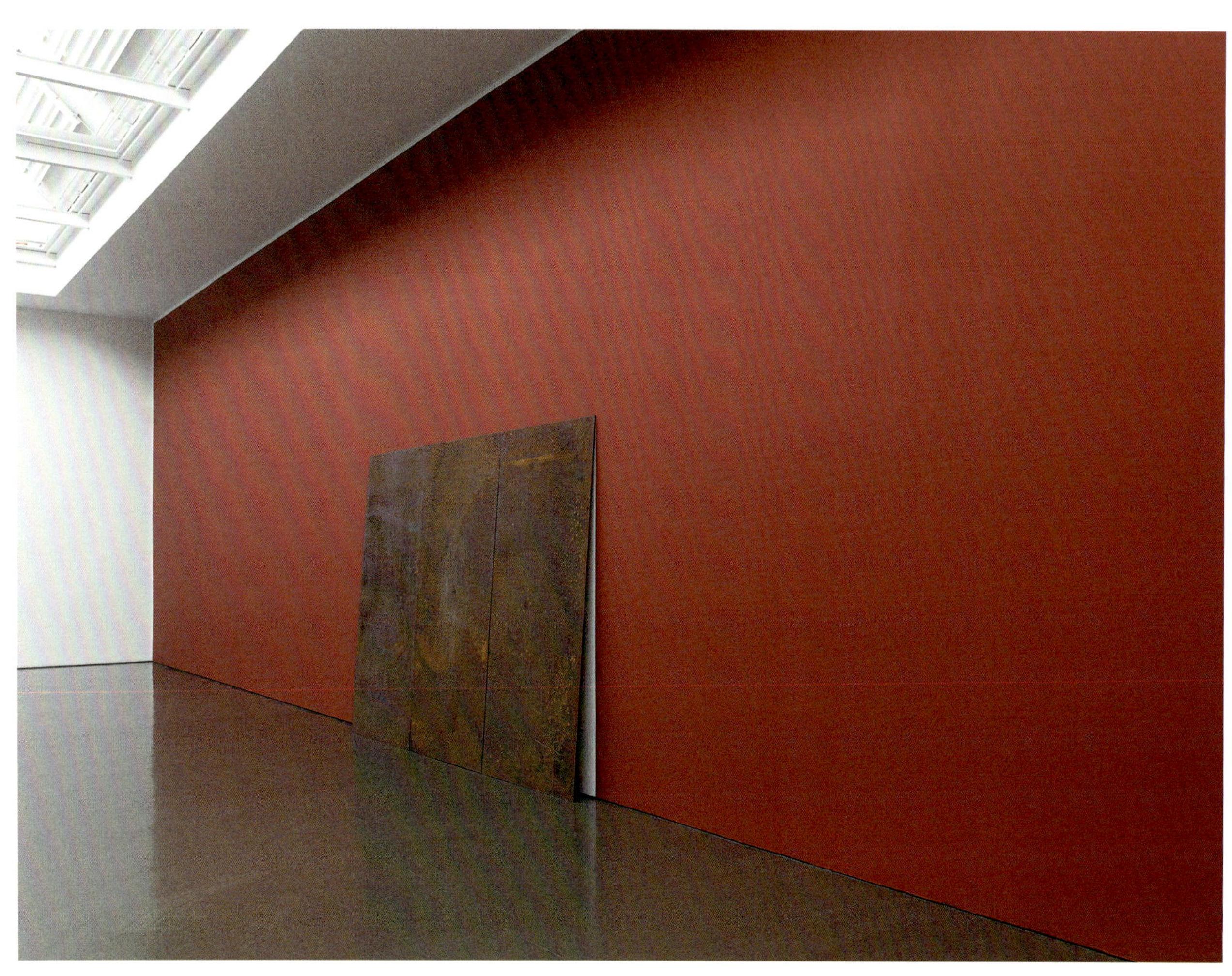

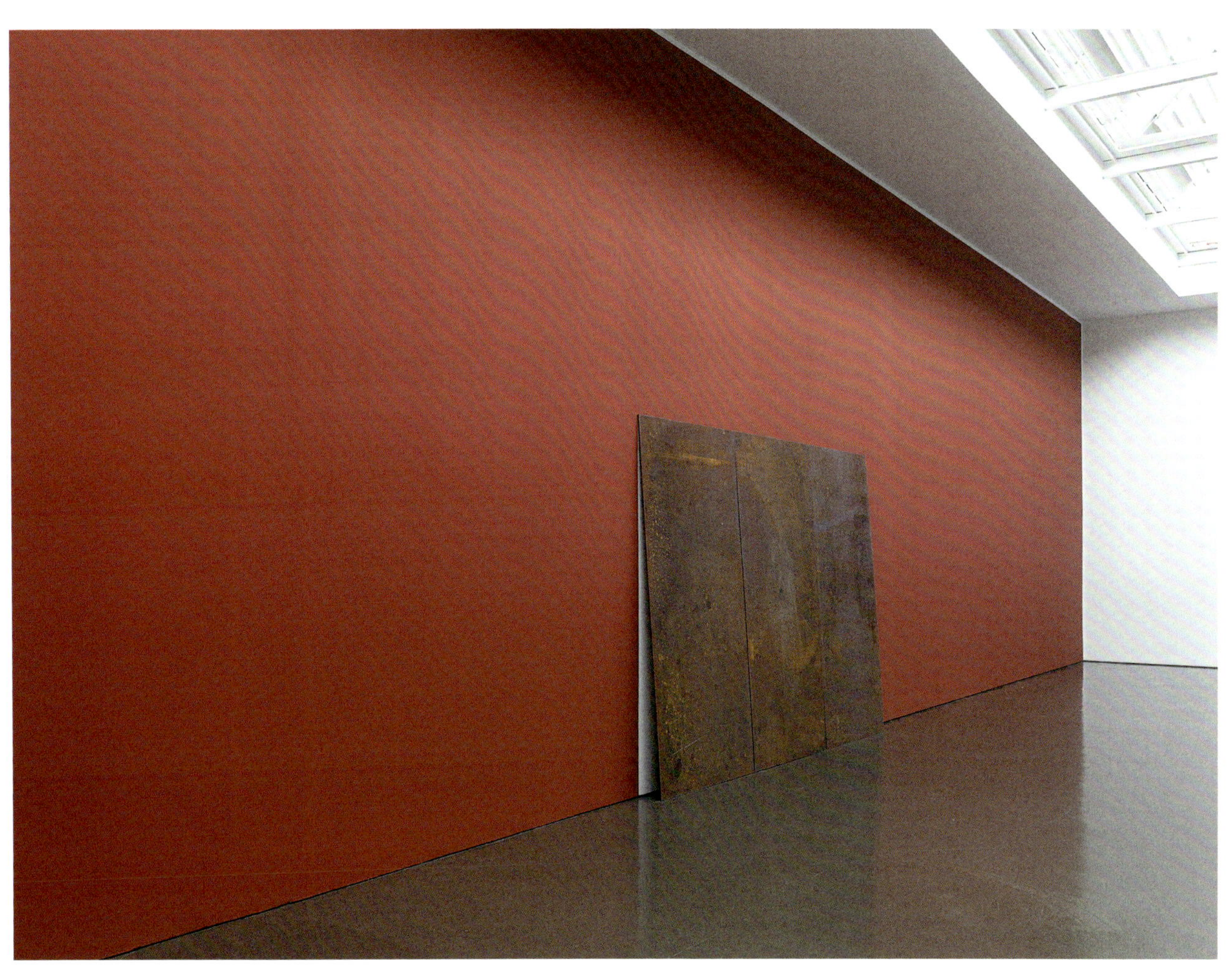

**Lili Dujourie**
Amerikaans Imperialism, 1972–2016

Reinhard Mucha

# Reinhard Mucha

**Reinhard Mucha**
O.T. – Oberer Totpunkt, T.D.C. – Top Dead Center, [1989] 1985

Probestück, Studio Piece, 1982

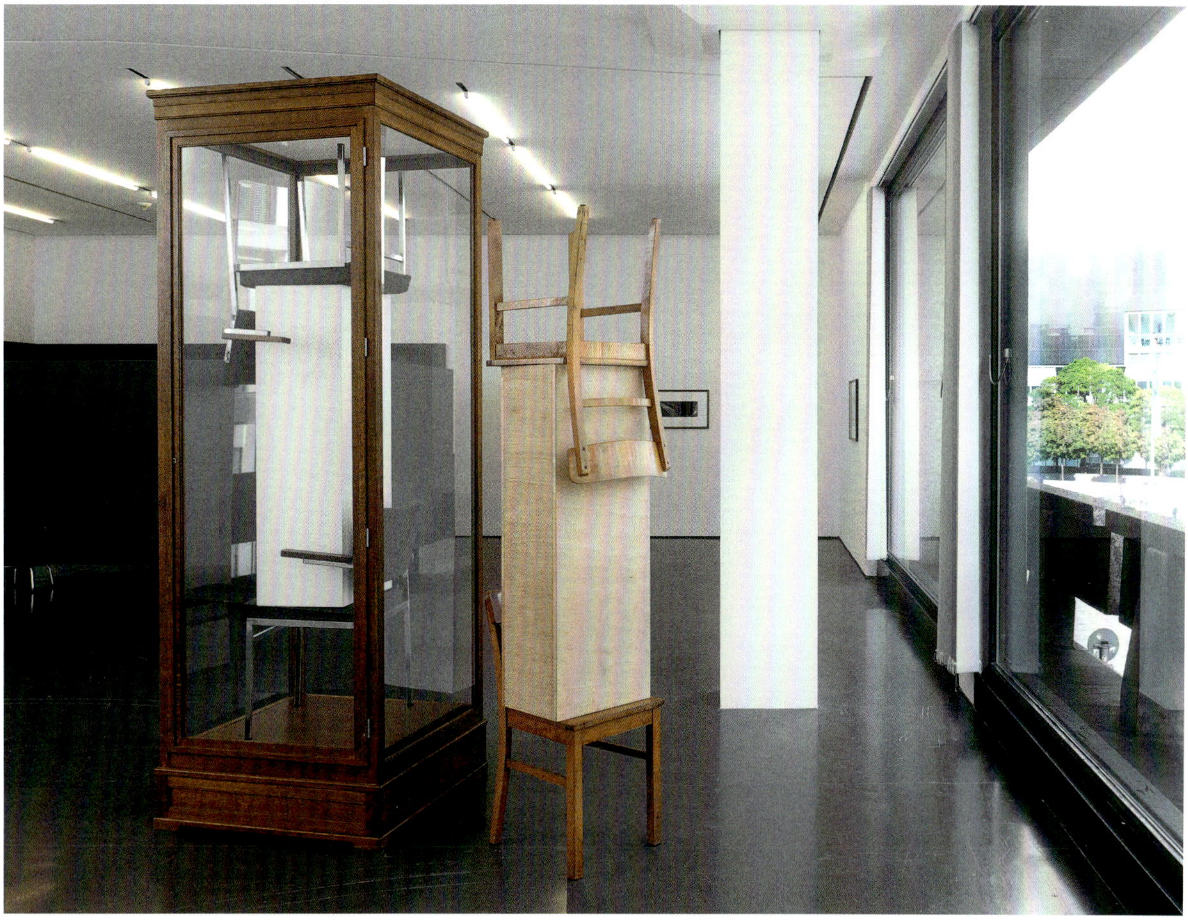

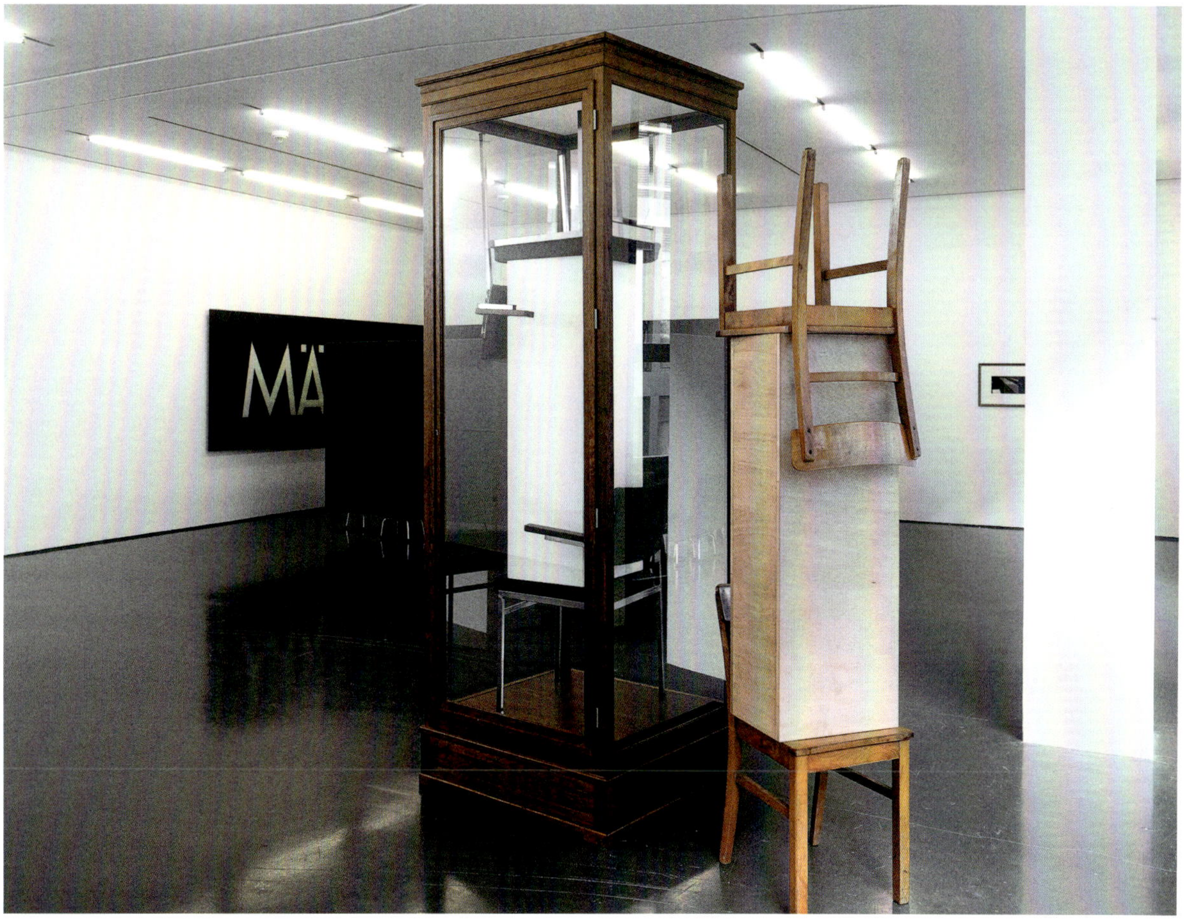

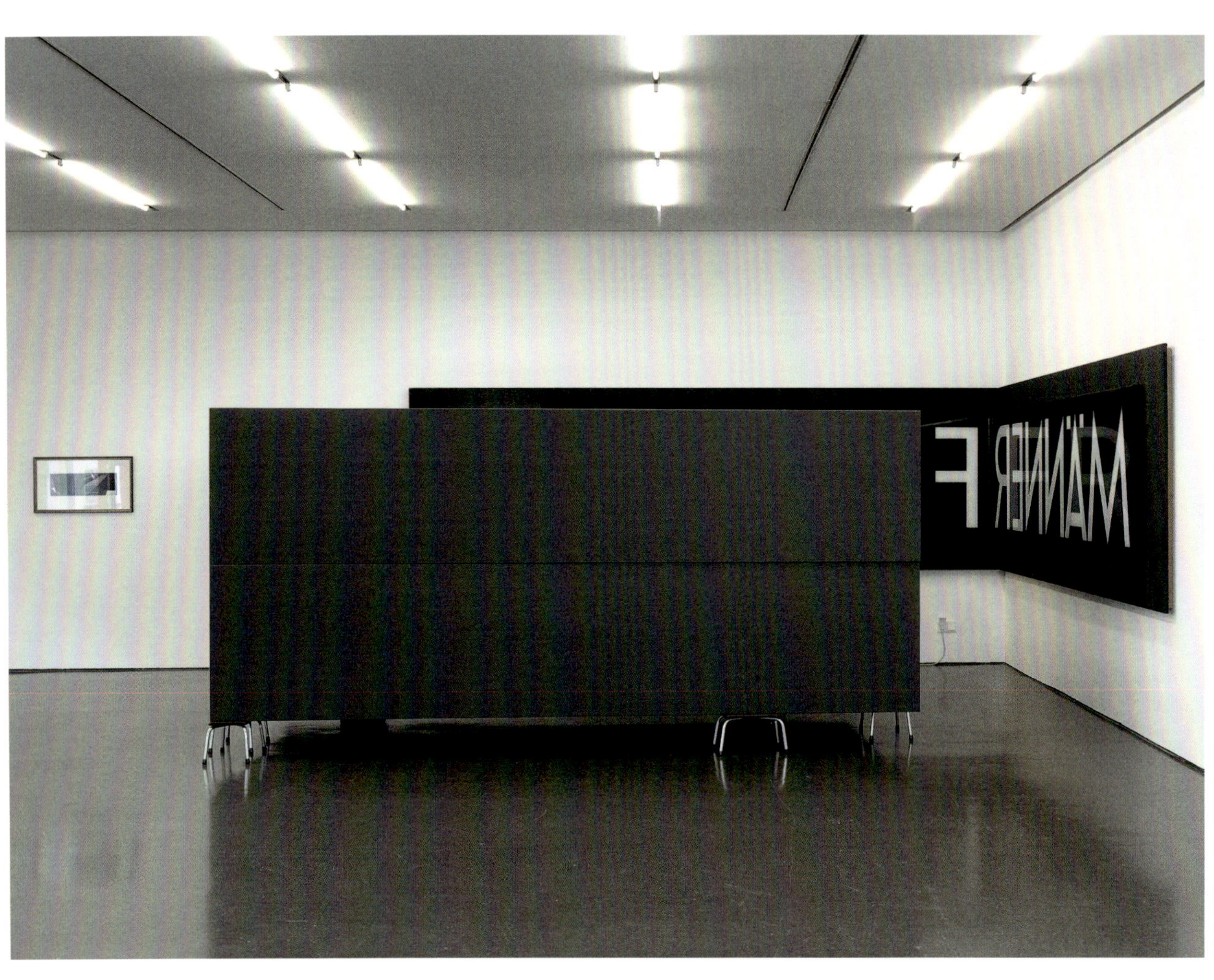
MÄNNER F

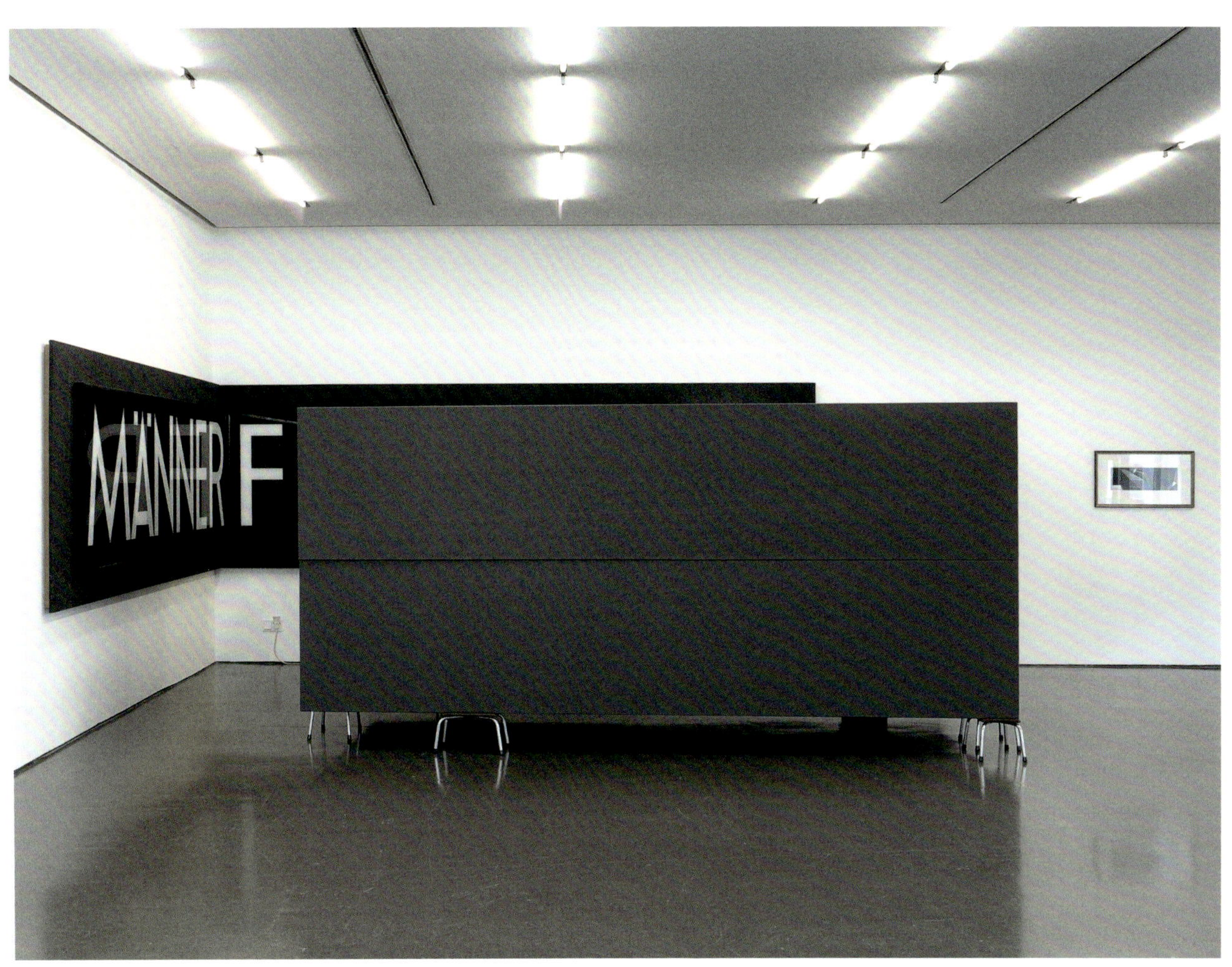


**Reinhard Mucha**
Oderin / Ohne Titel (MÄNNER FRAUEN), [1987] 1987 / 1981
2-teiliges Werkensemble

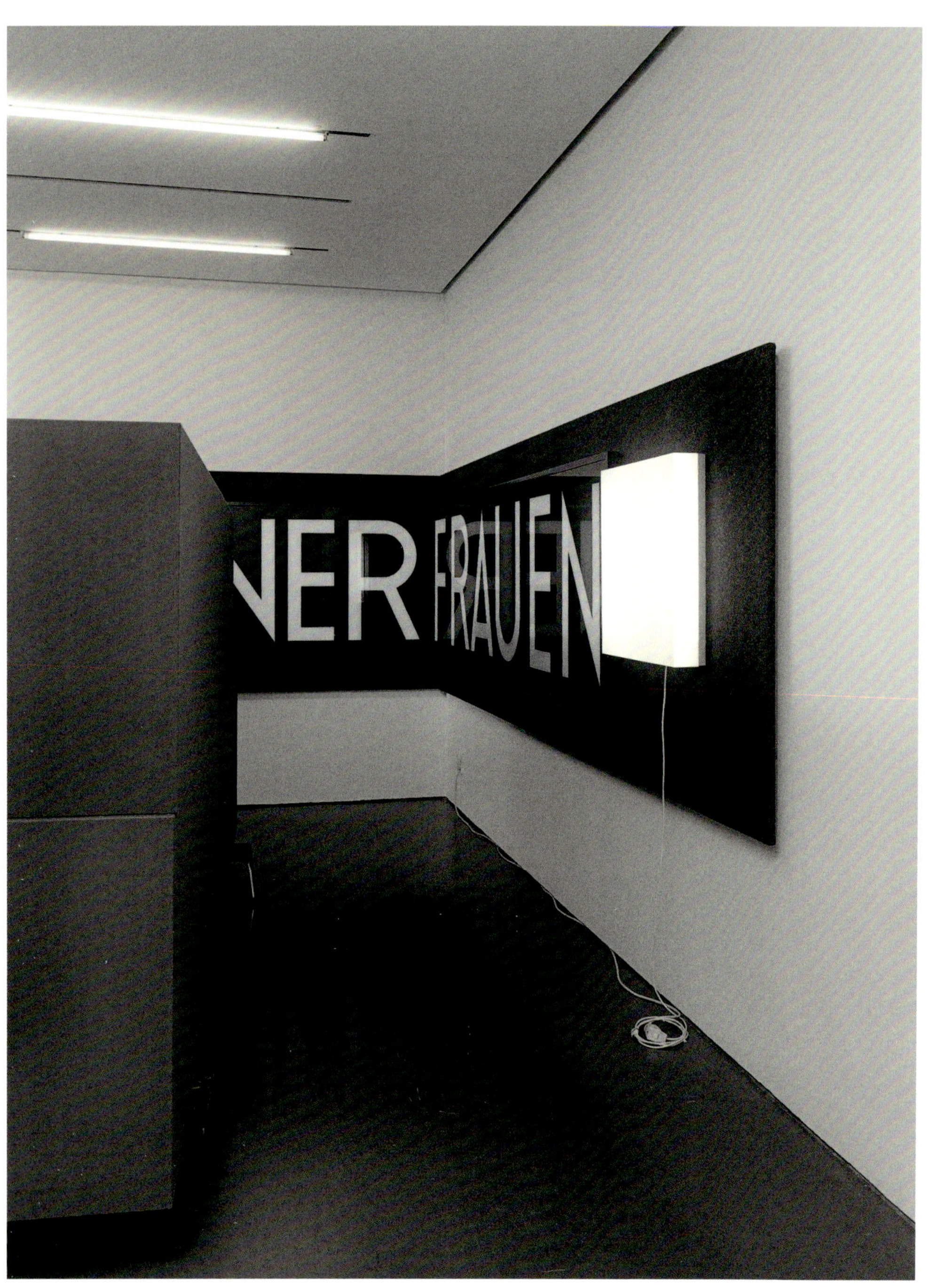


**Reinhard Mucha**
Oderin / Ohne Titel (MÄNNER FRAUEN), [1987] 1987 / 1981
2-teiliges Werkensemble

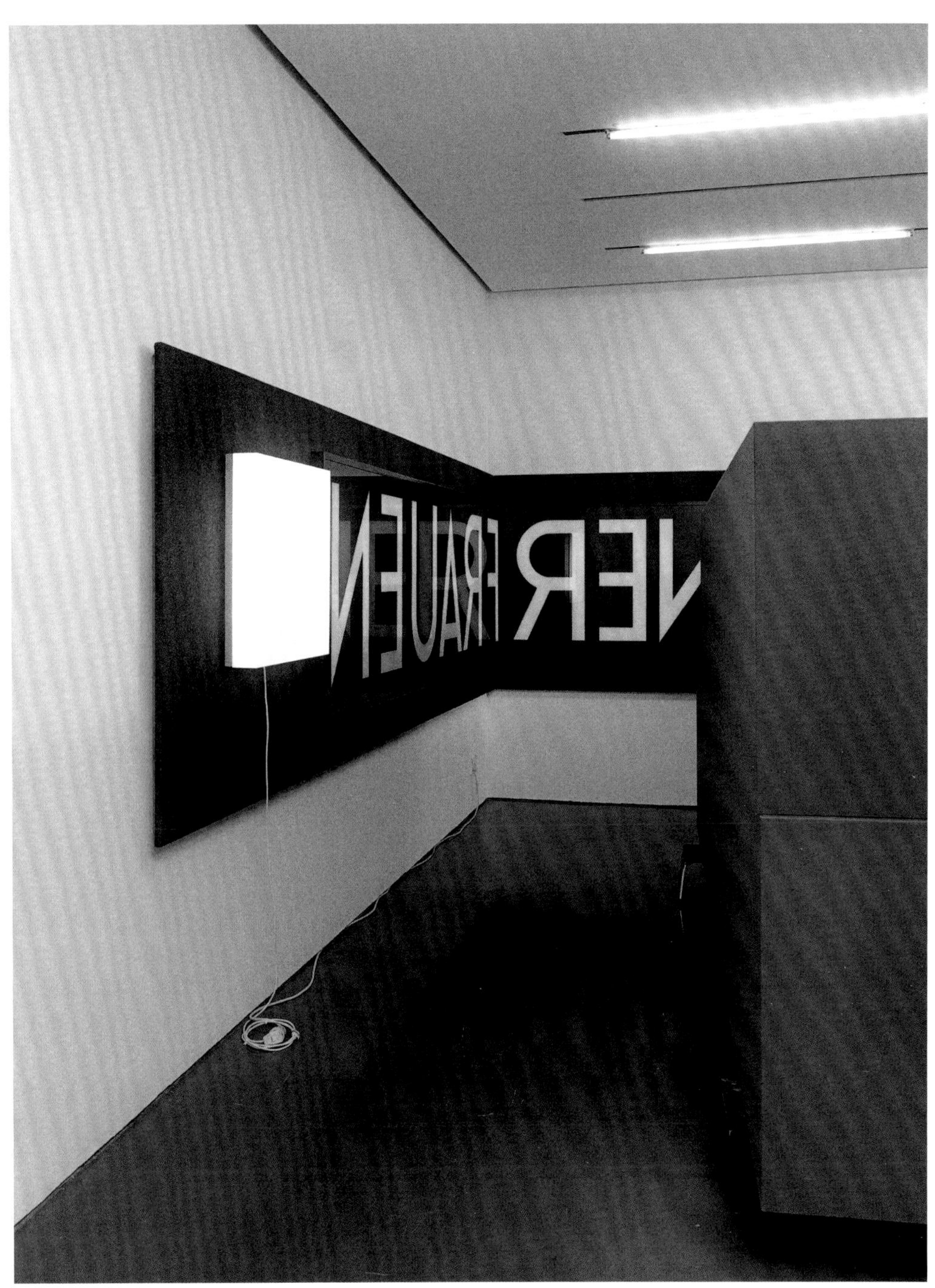

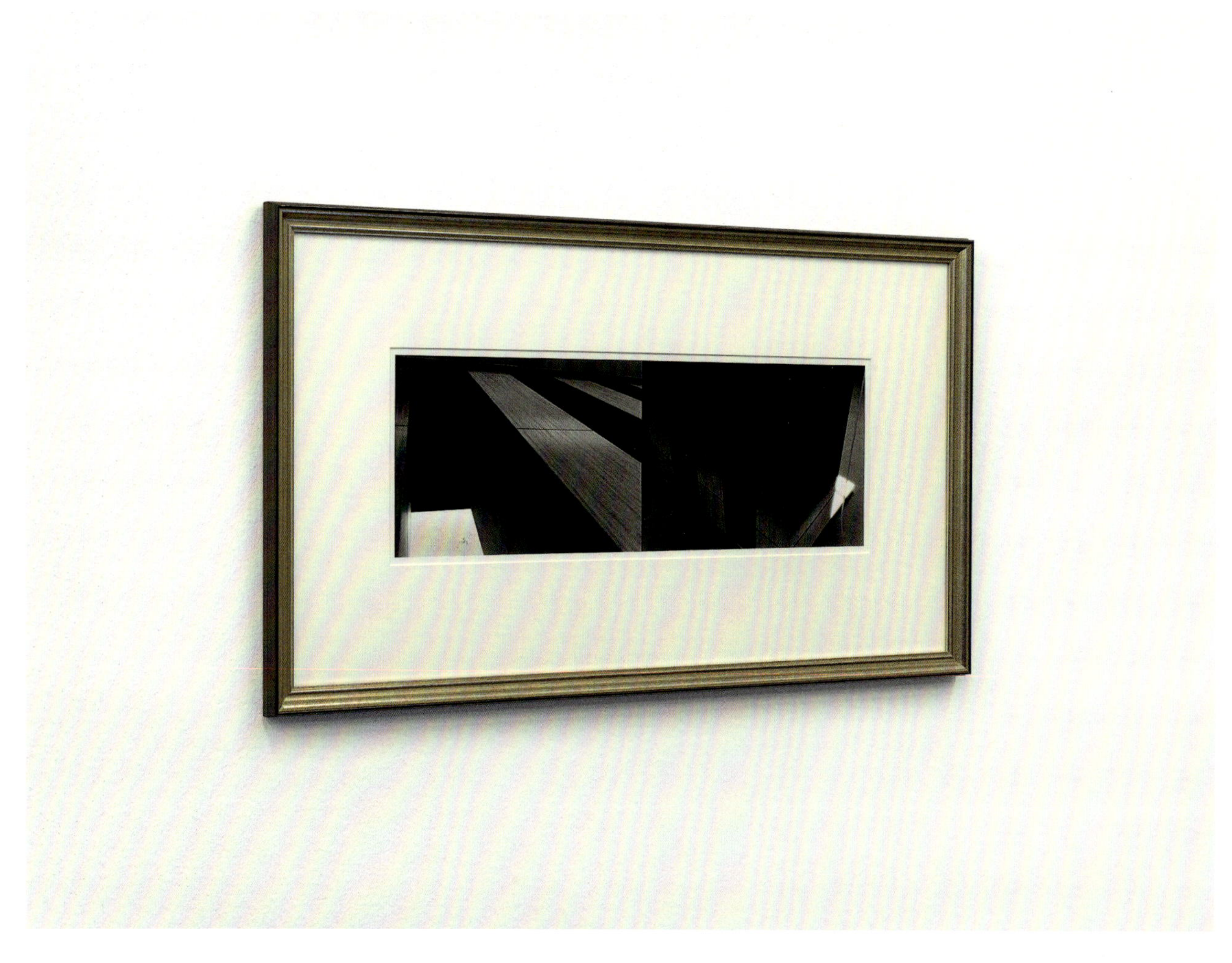

**Reinhard Mucha**
Zwei Photos ohne Titel [Ohne Titel (Oberhausen)],
[2003] 1983

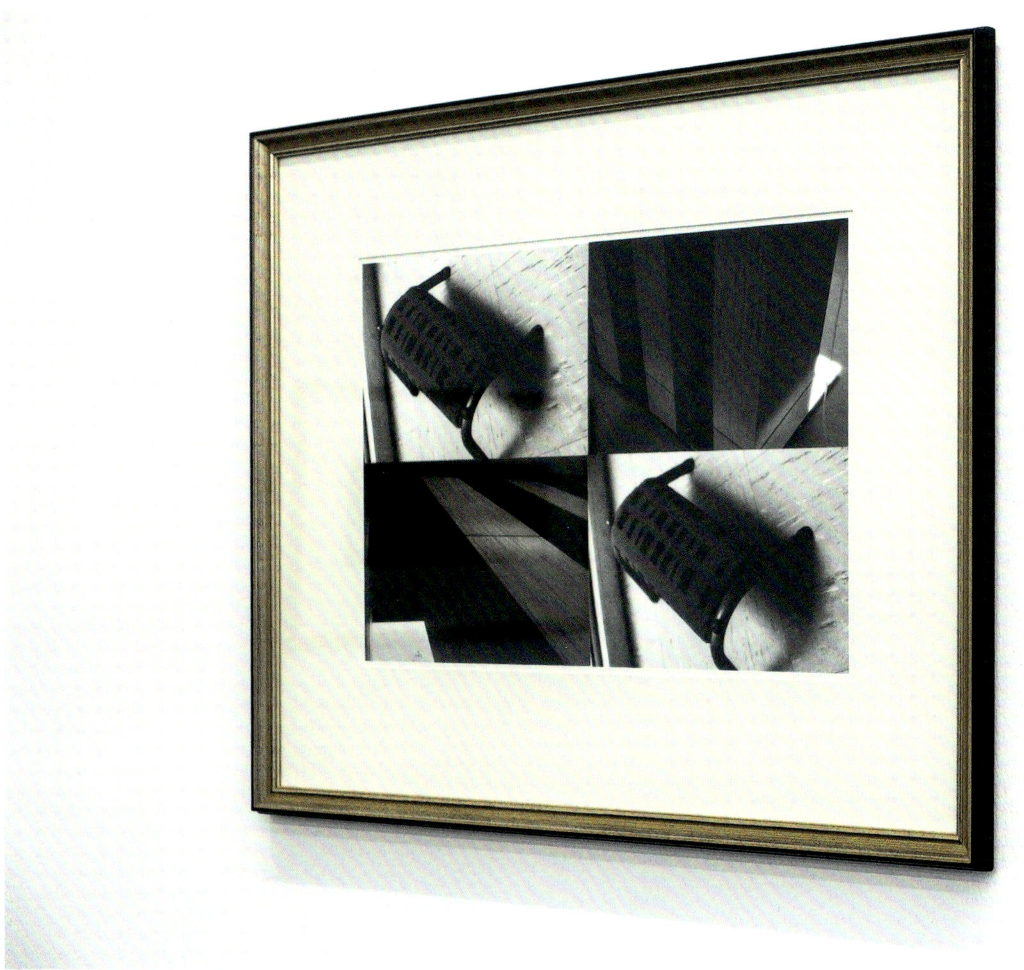

**Reinhard Mucha**
Vier Photos ohne Titel [Ohne Titel (Oberhausen) / Urlaub im All],
[2003] 1983/1988

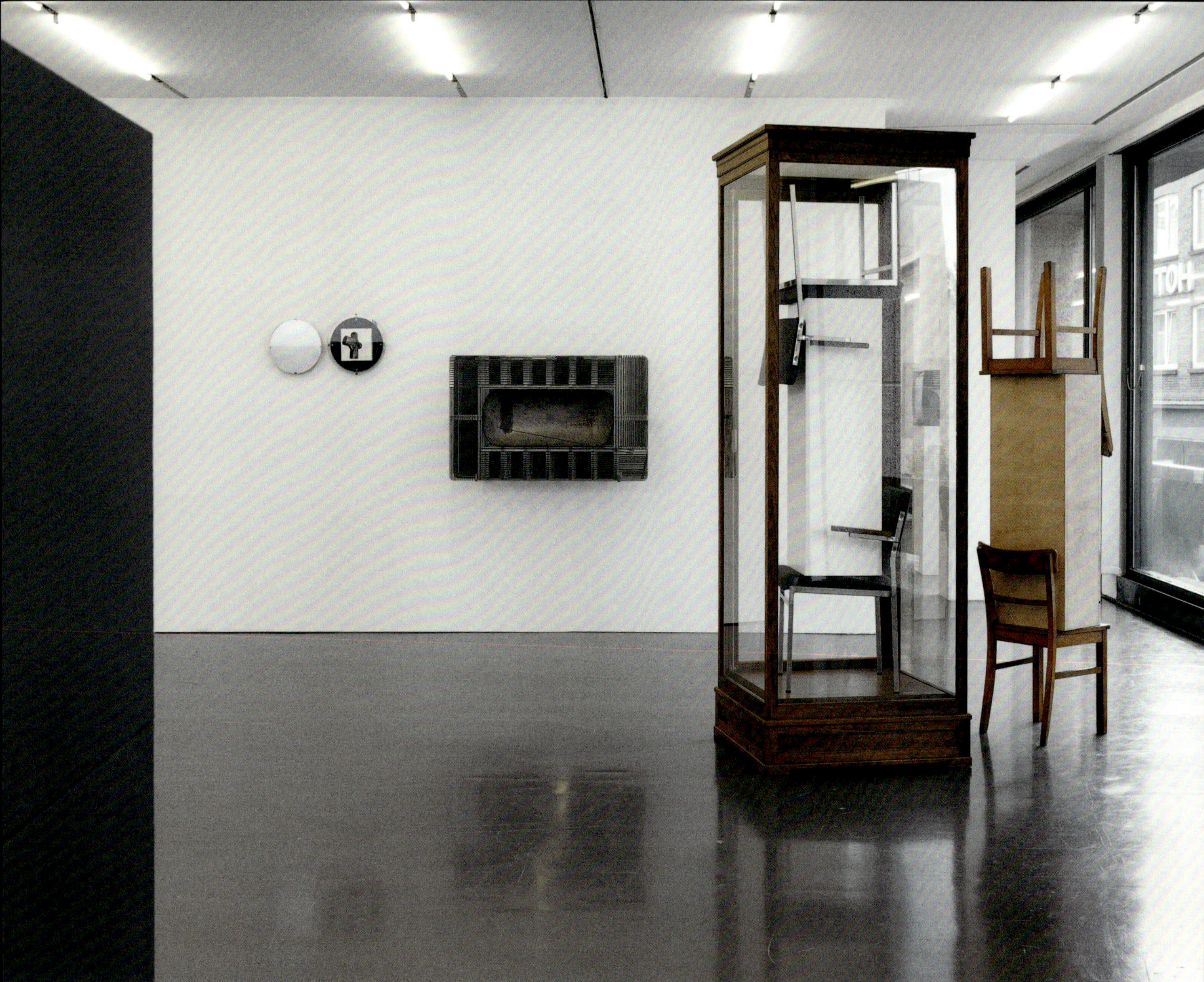

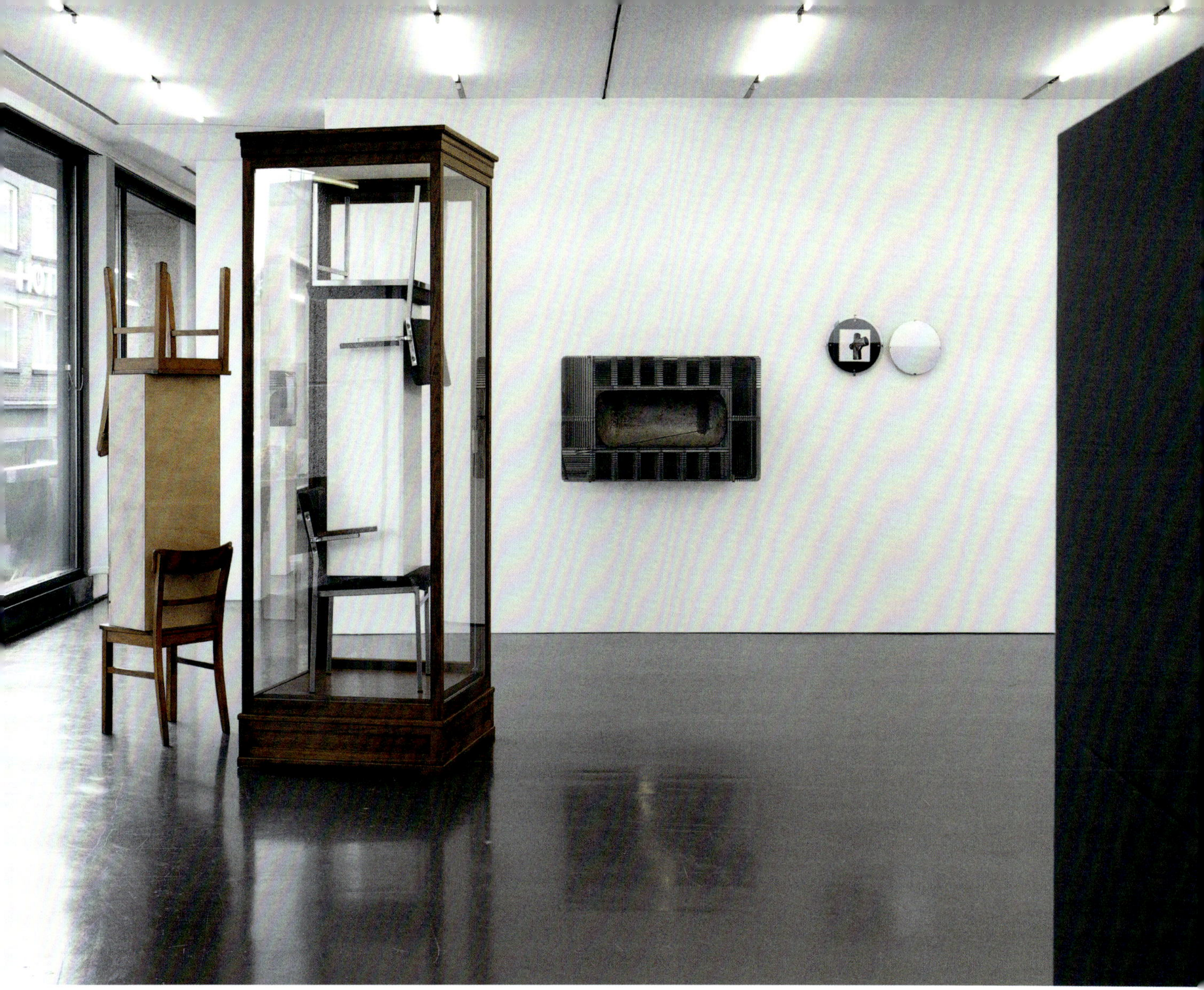

**Reinhard Mucha**
Probestück, Studio Piece, 1982

O.T. – Oberer Totpunkt, T.D.C. – Top Dead Center, [1989] 1985

Werden, 2016

Edition 1991 – >>Kreuzstück<<, 2004

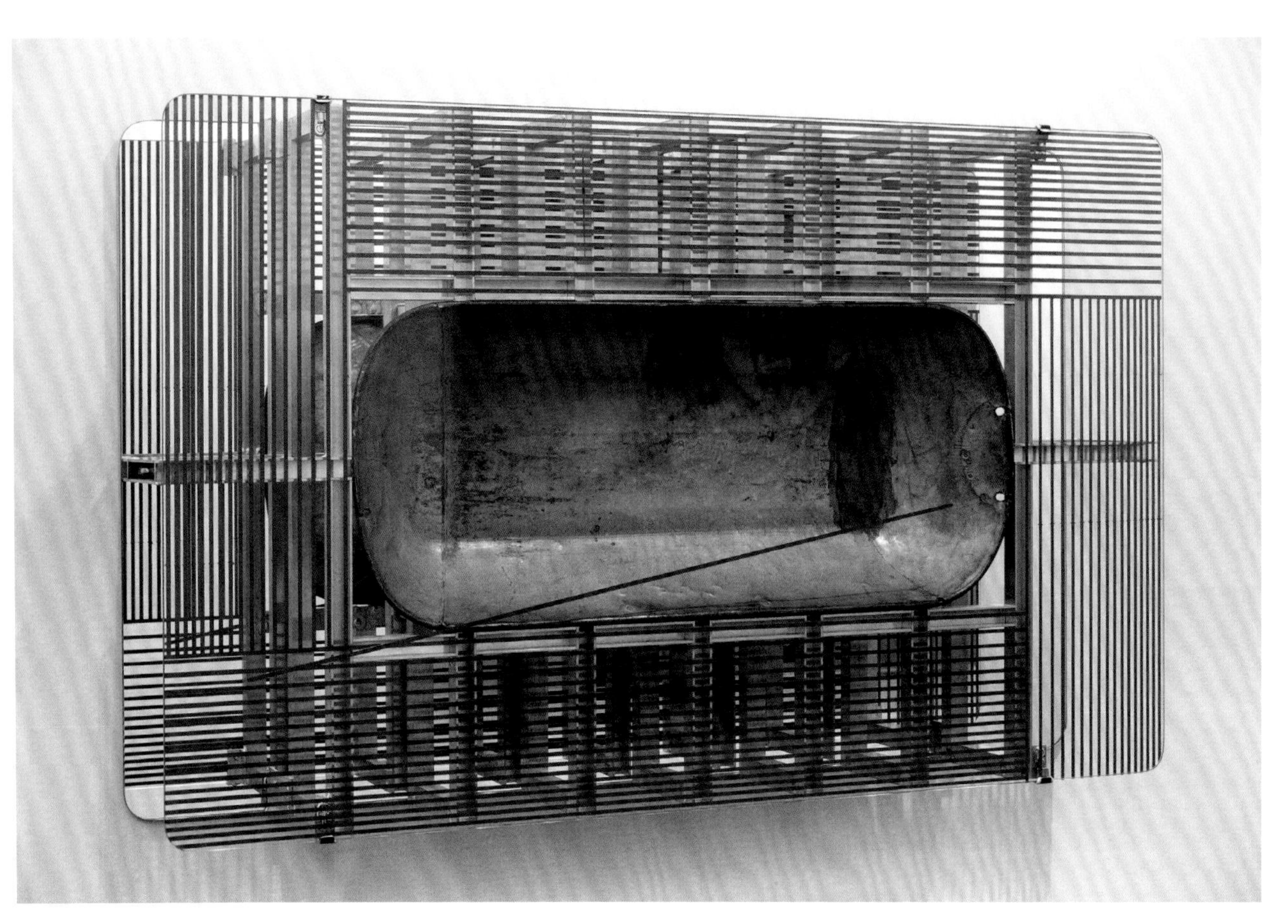

**Reinhard Mucha**
Werden, 2016

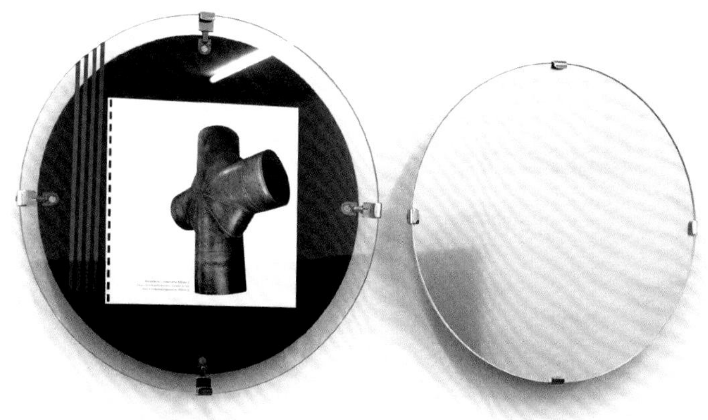

**Reinhard Mucha**
Edition 1991 – >>Kreuzstück<<, 2004

# Sturtevant

# Sturtevant

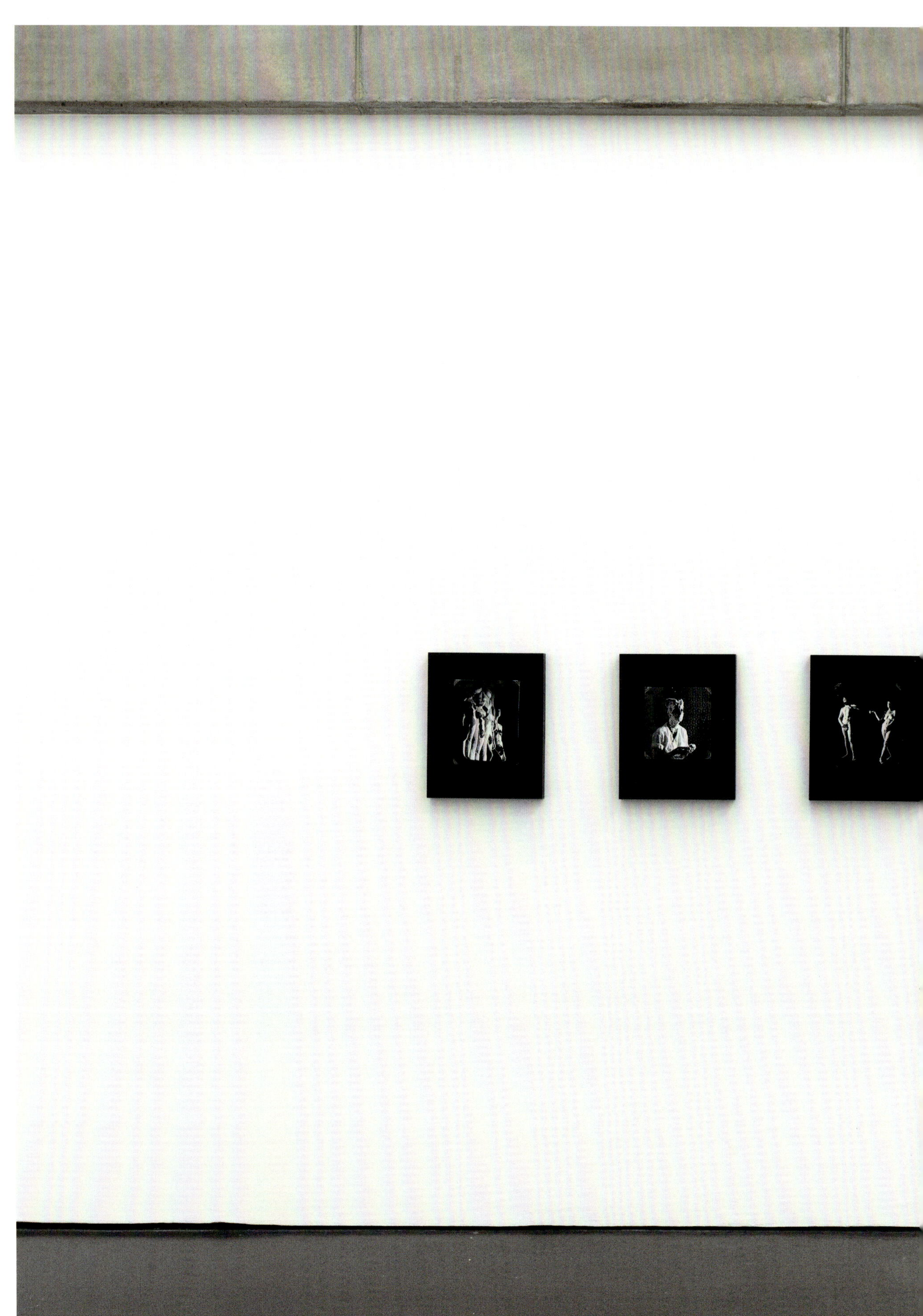

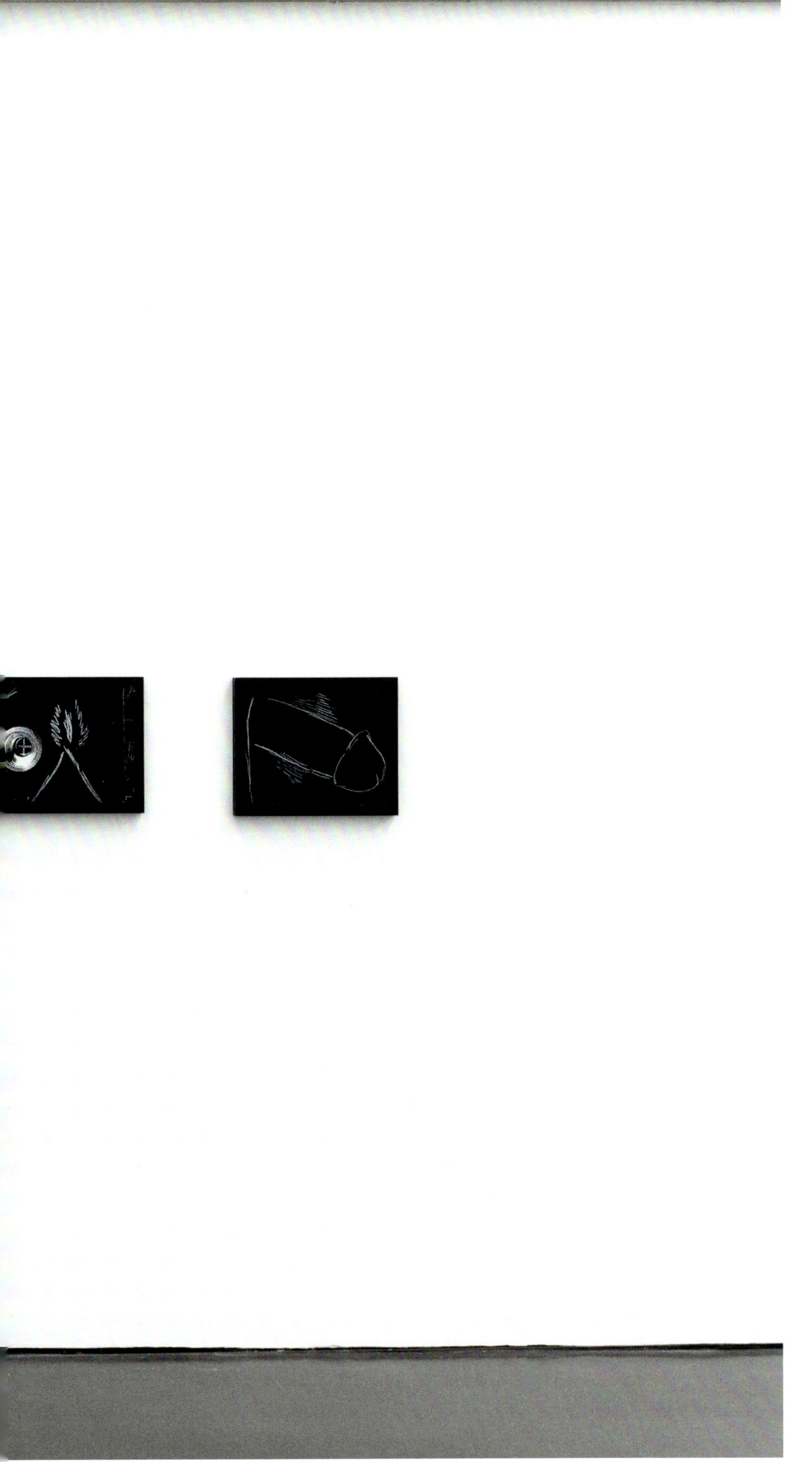

**Elaine Sturtevant**
Duchamp – Nu descendant un escalier, 1968

Duchamp – Man Ray Portrait, 1966

Duchamp – Relâche, 1967

Scale Model for Gober Wall Paper, 1994

Study for Gober Dick Paper, 1994

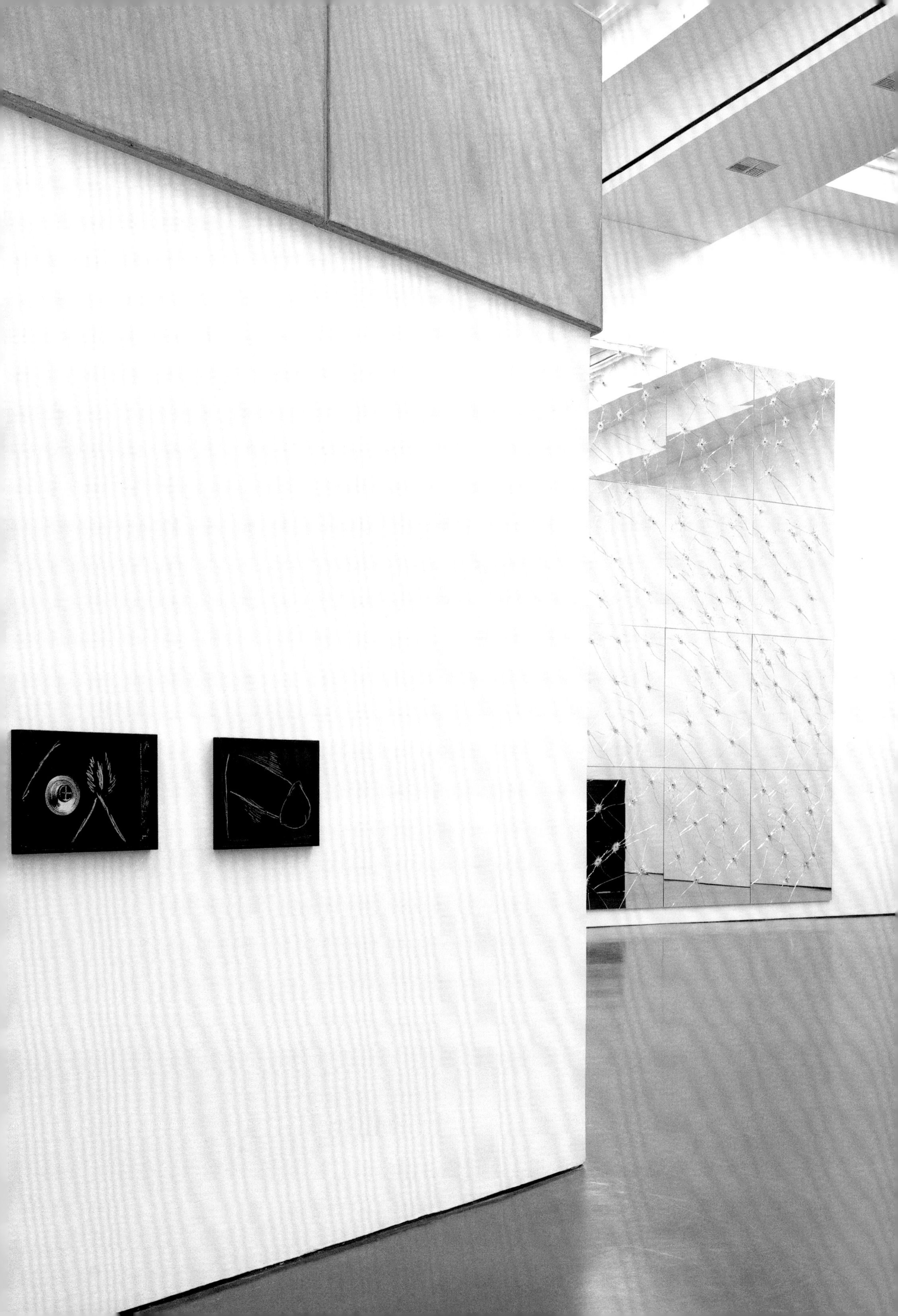

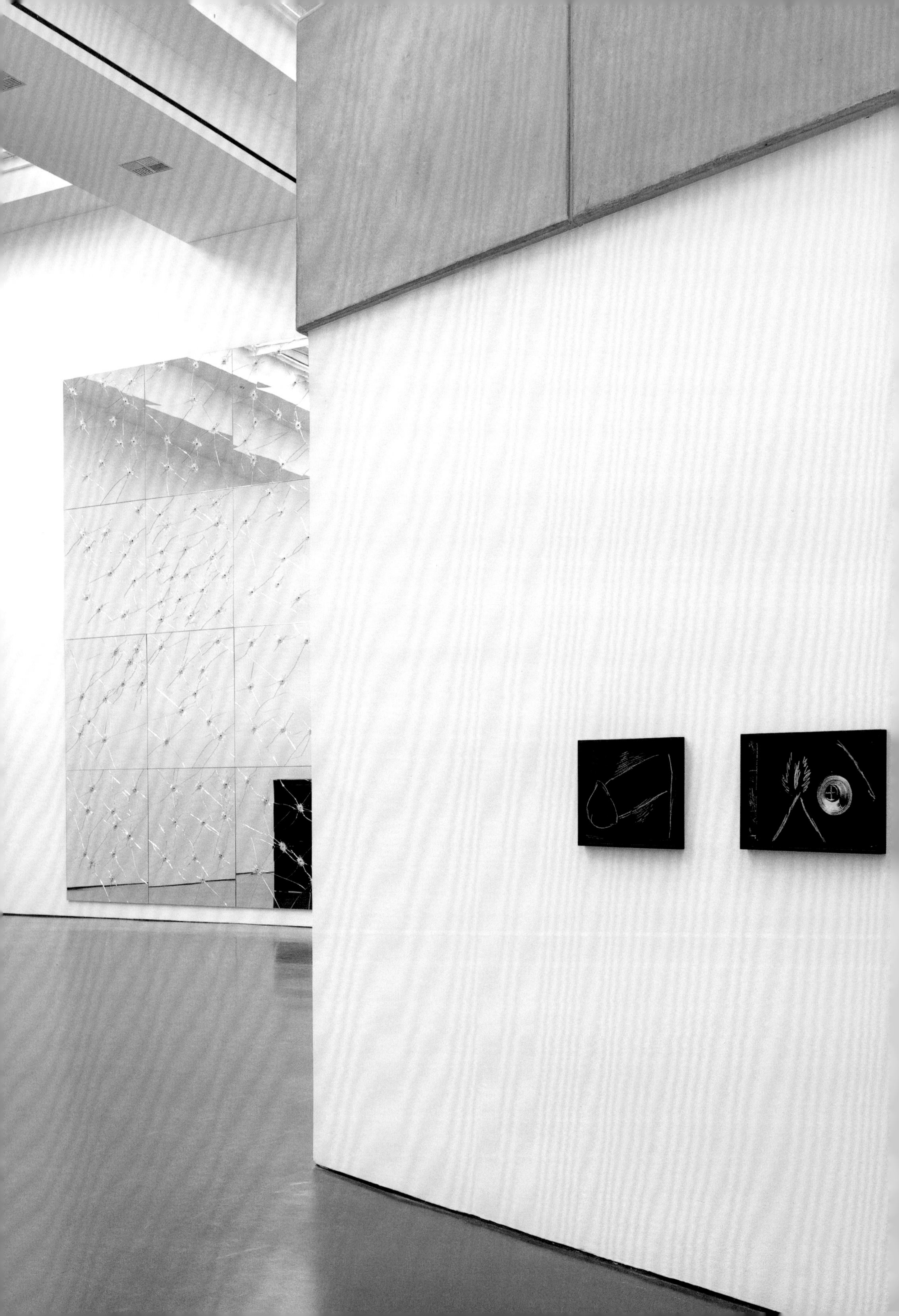

# Astrid Klein

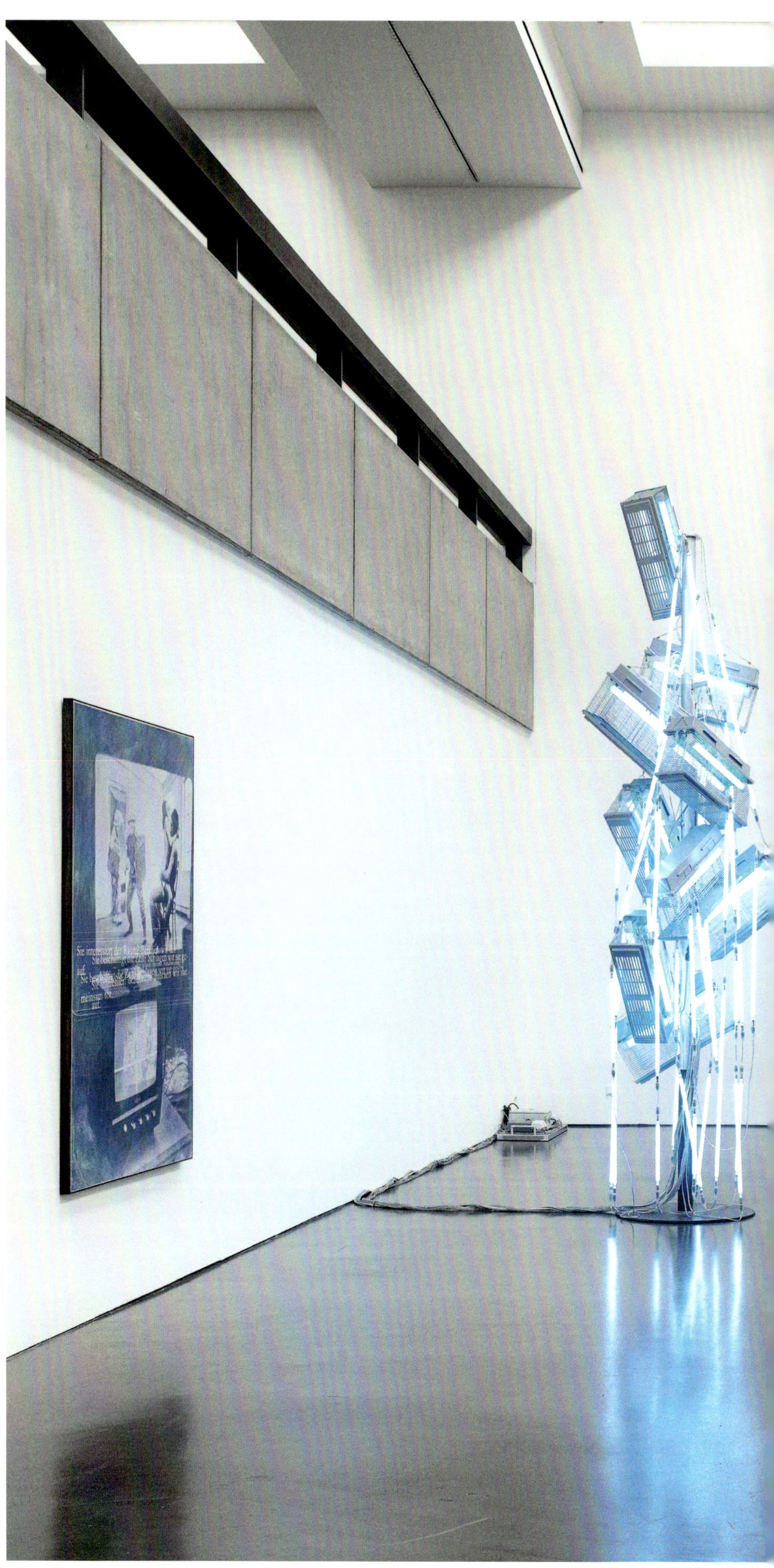

**Astrid Klein**
Ohne Titel (Sie interessiert der Raum?...), 1979

Fly Catcher III, 1987–91

Untitled, 1993/2011

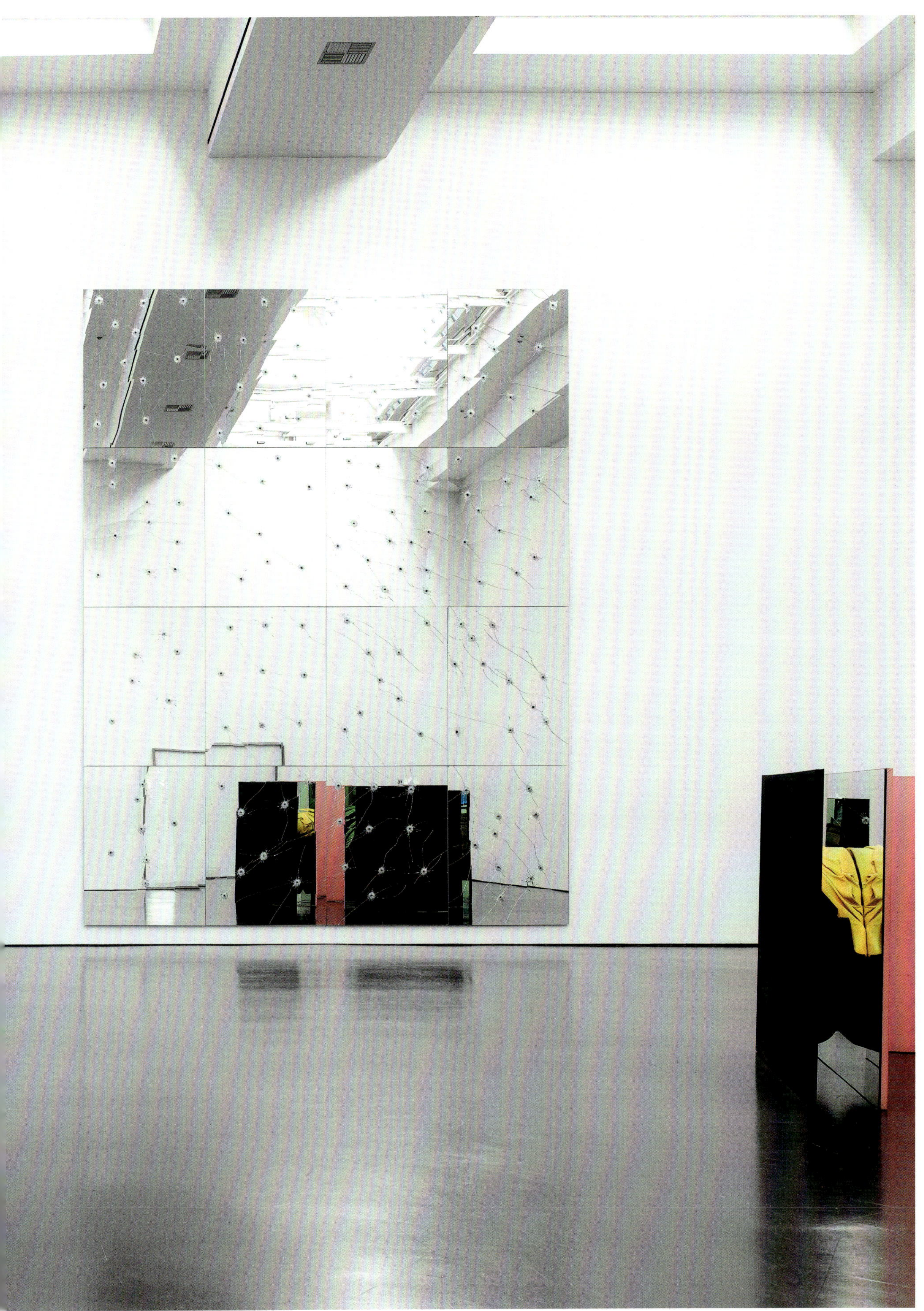

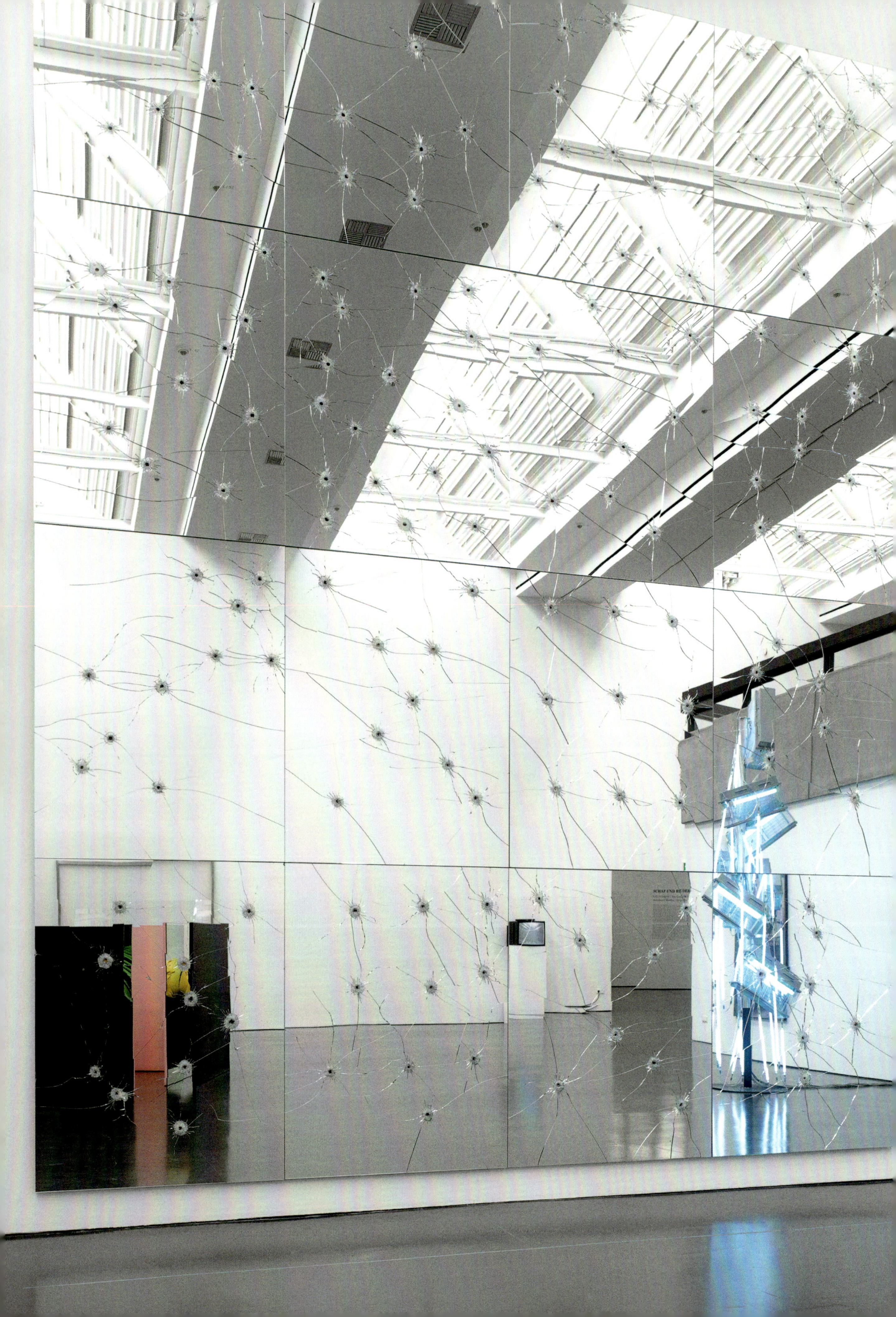
SCHAF UND

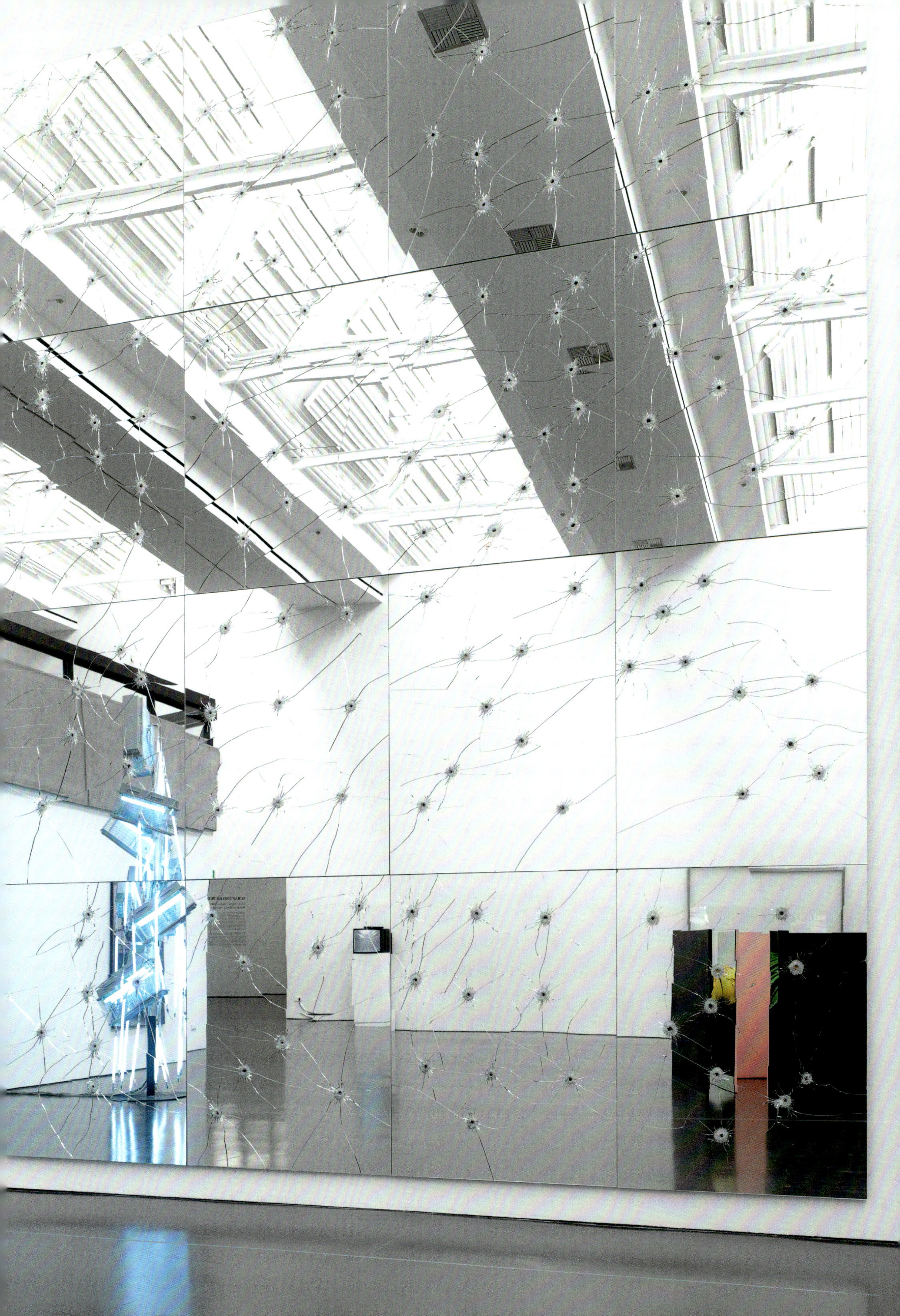

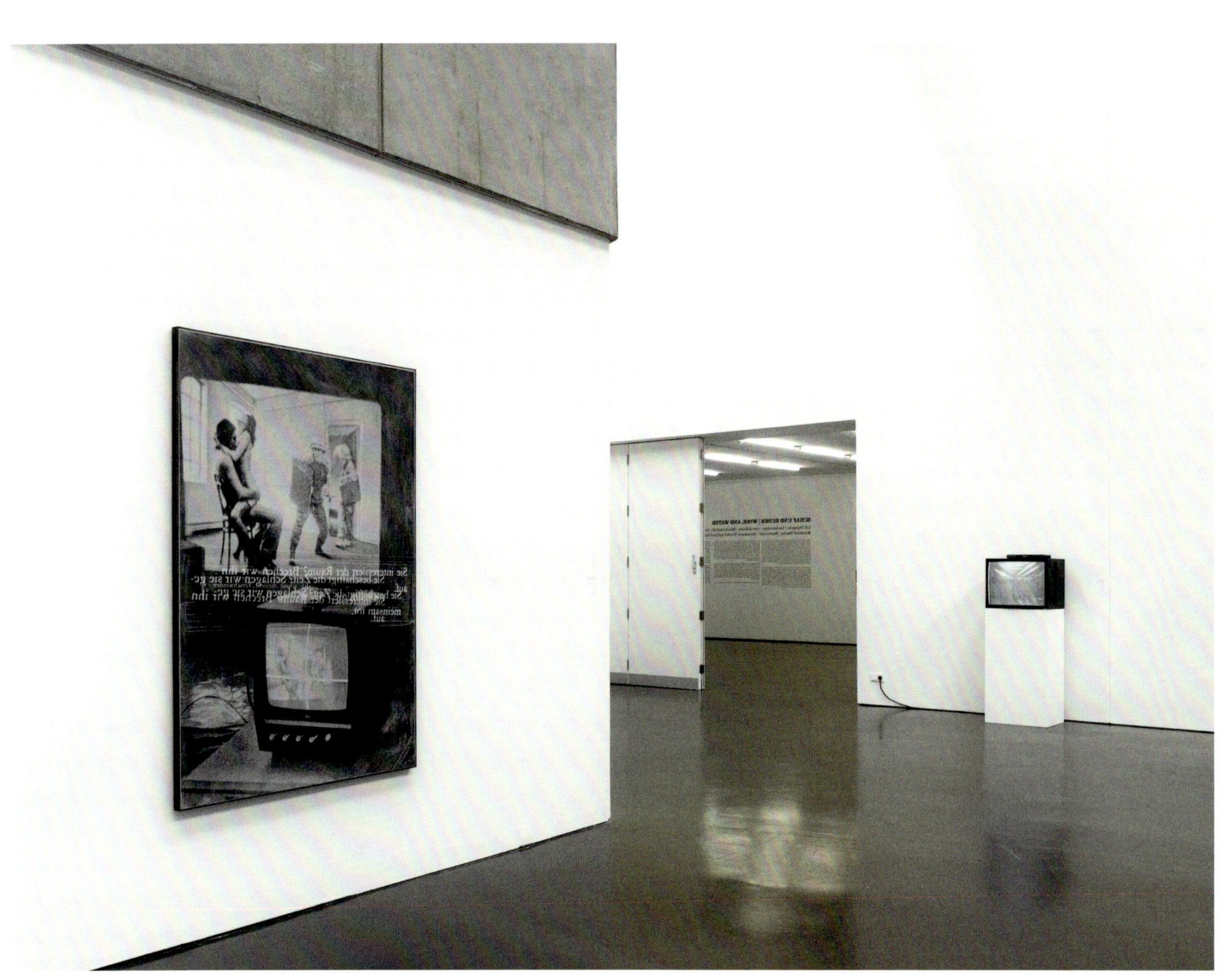

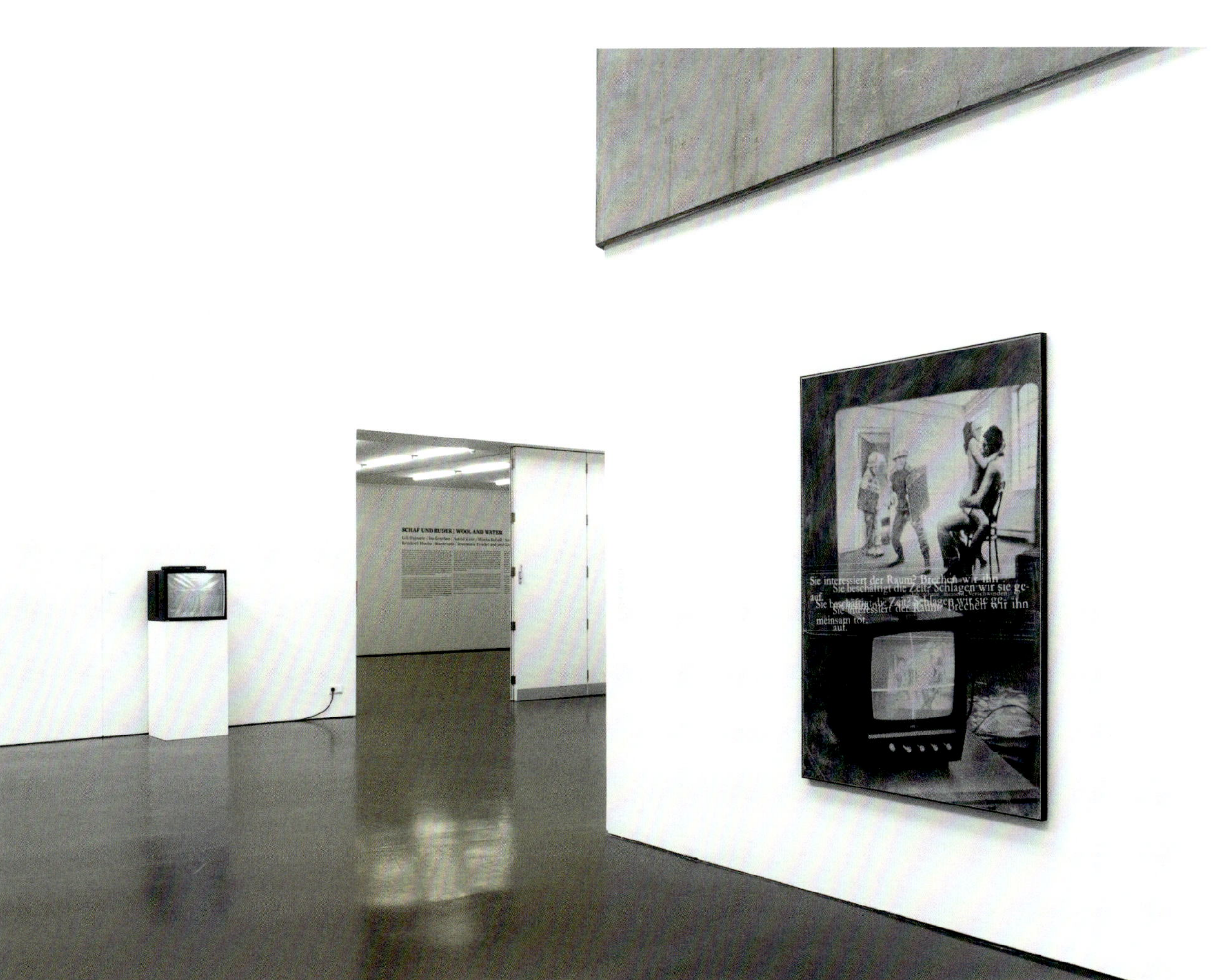


**Astrid Klein**
Ohne Titel (Sie interessiert der Raum?...), 1979

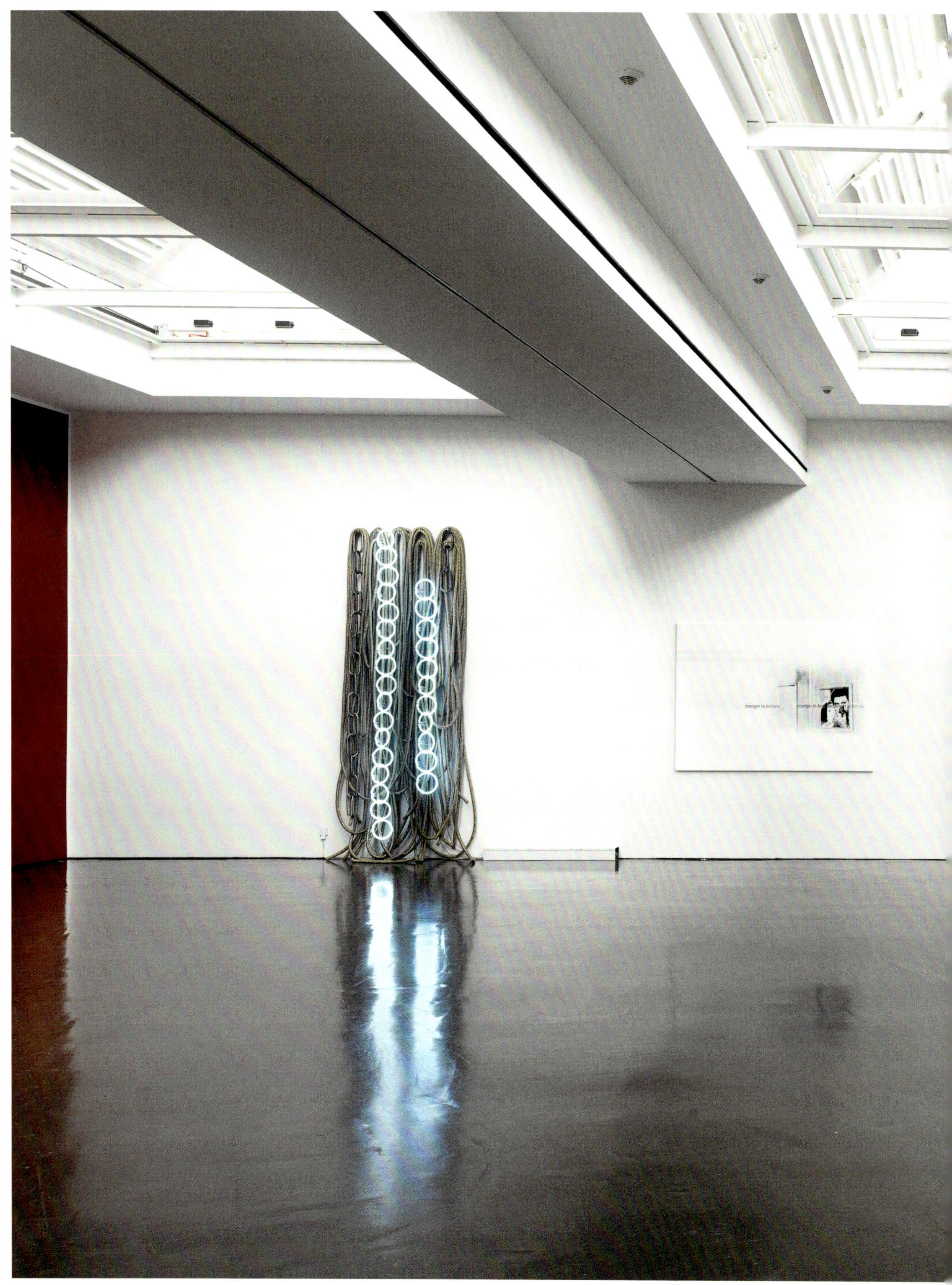

**Astrid Klein**
Untitled (Wie kommt die Zeit ins Hirn, Centralnervös), 1998

Corriger la fortune (From the series of the white paintings), 1988

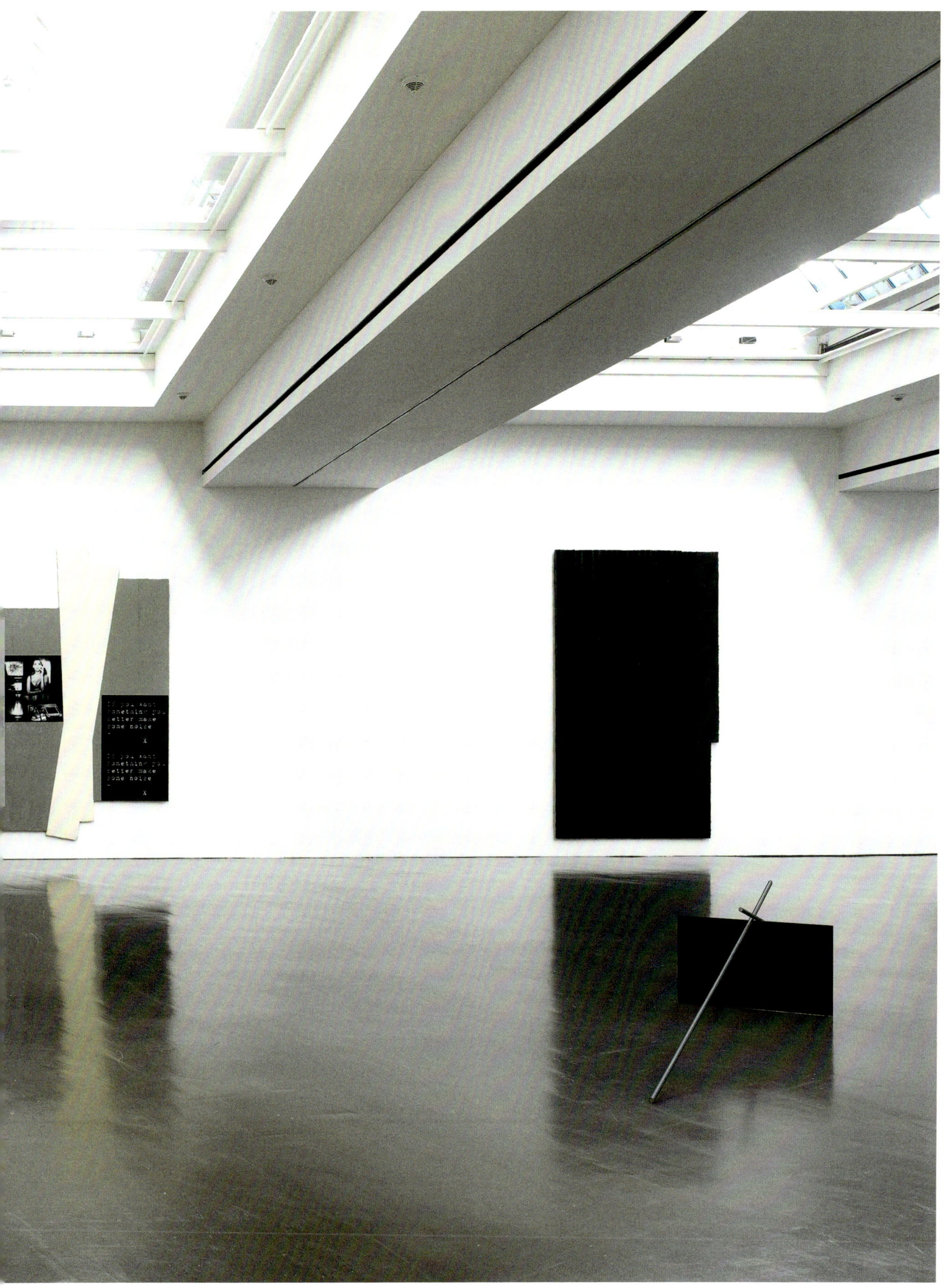

Untitled (If you want something … ), 2012

Untitled (Le spectacle n'arrête pas), 2012

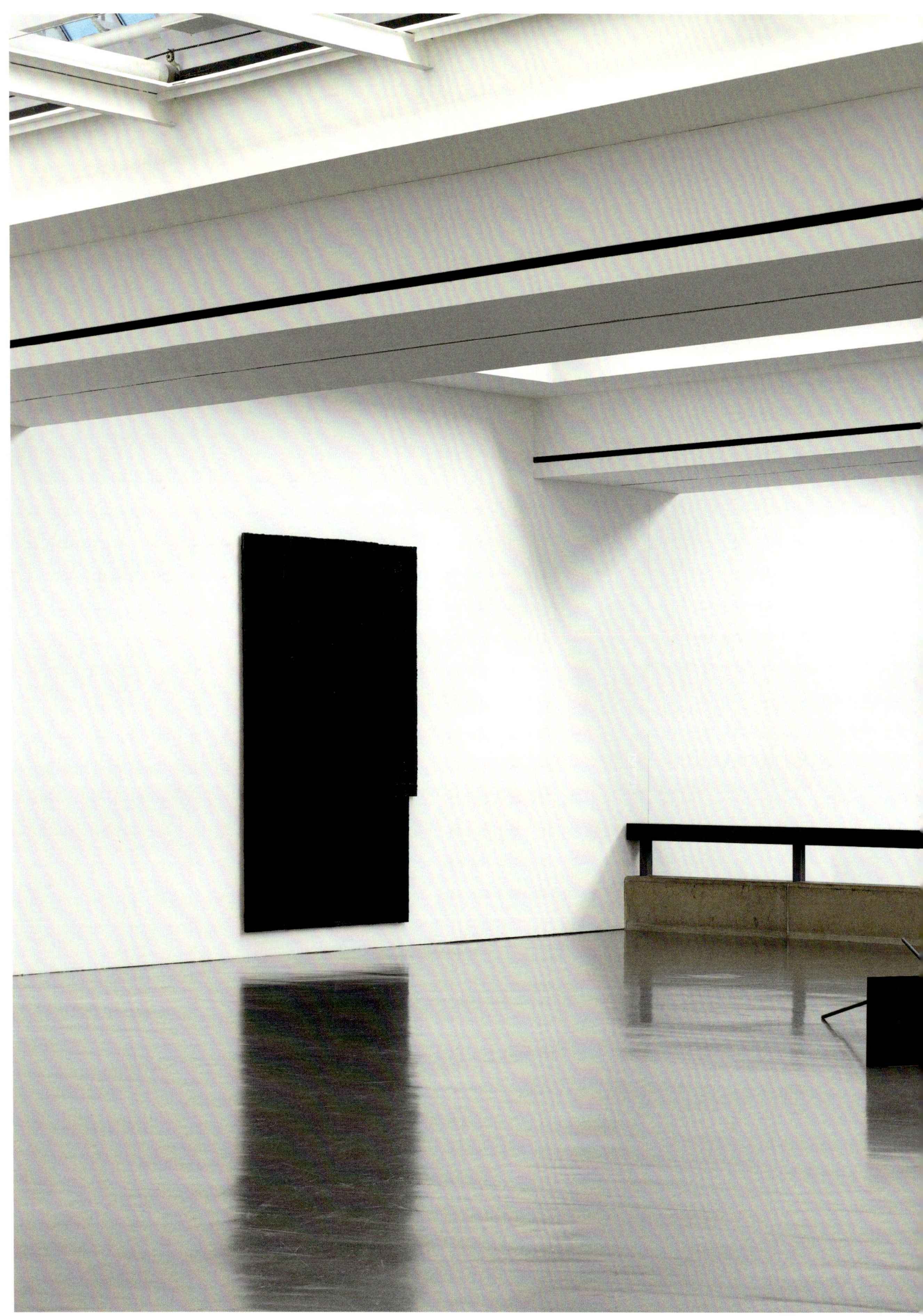

# Isa Genzken

# Isa Genzken

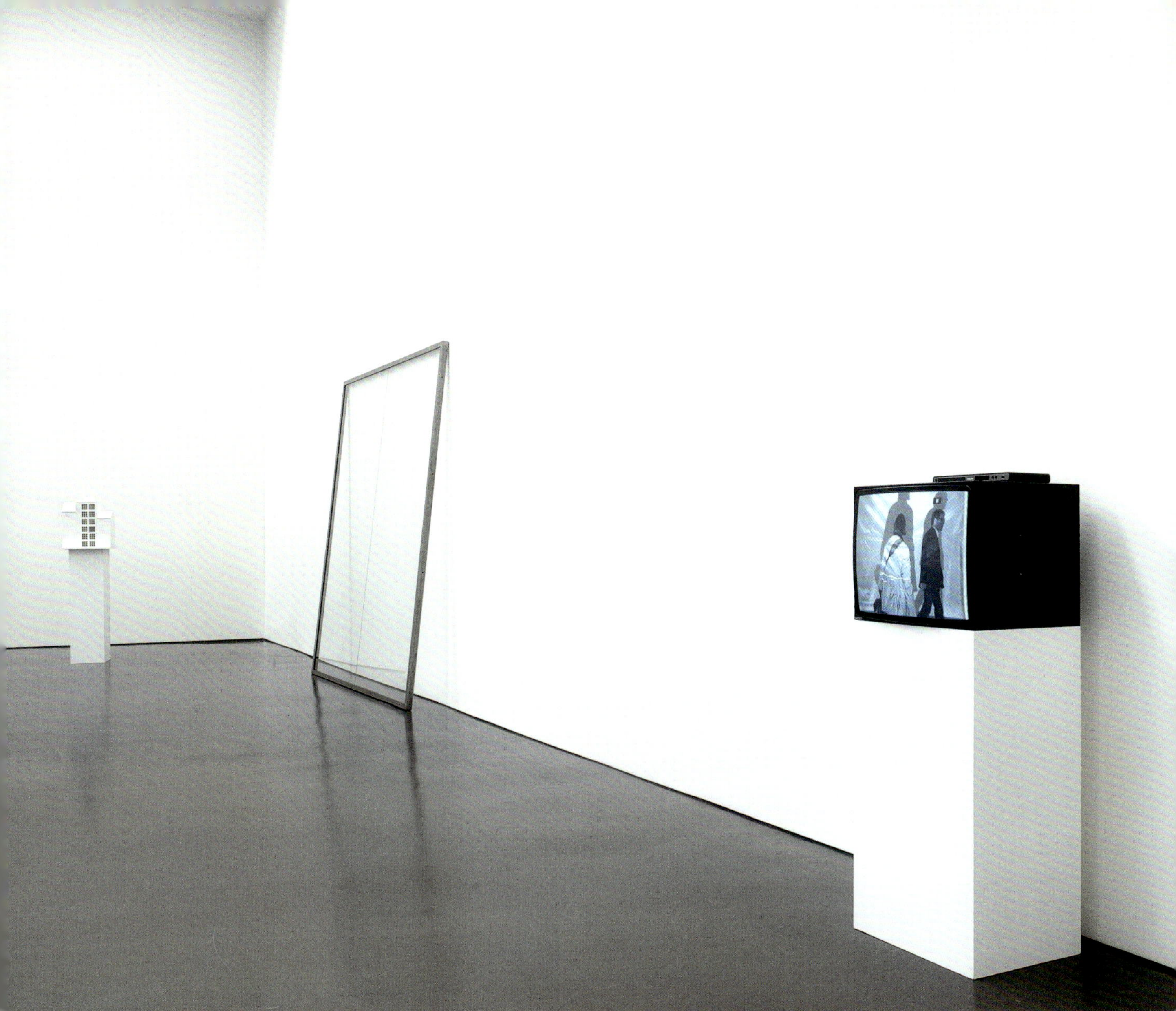

**Isa Genzken**
Fenster, Venloer Straße 21, 1988,
Model, 2015

Großes Fenster, 1987/88

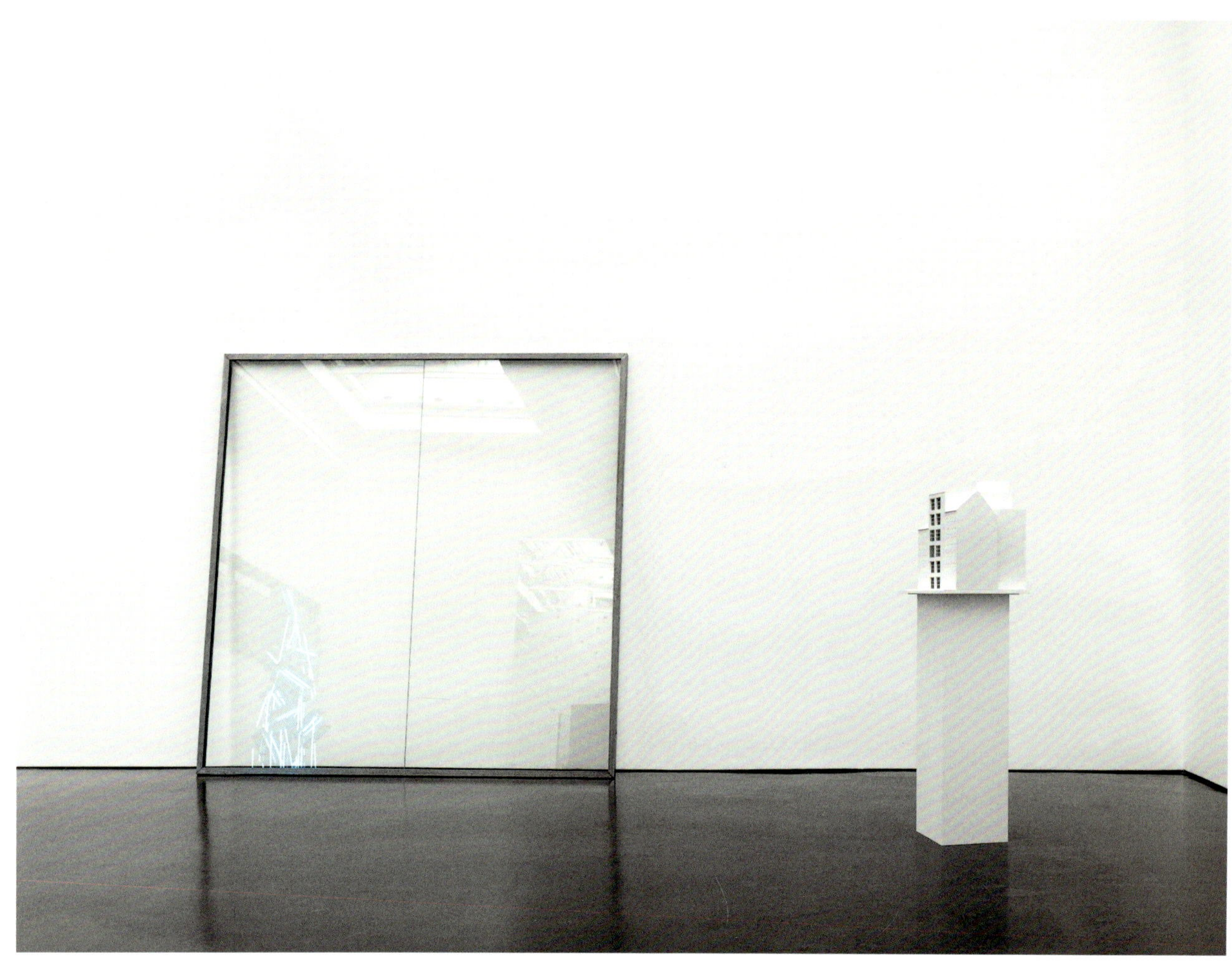

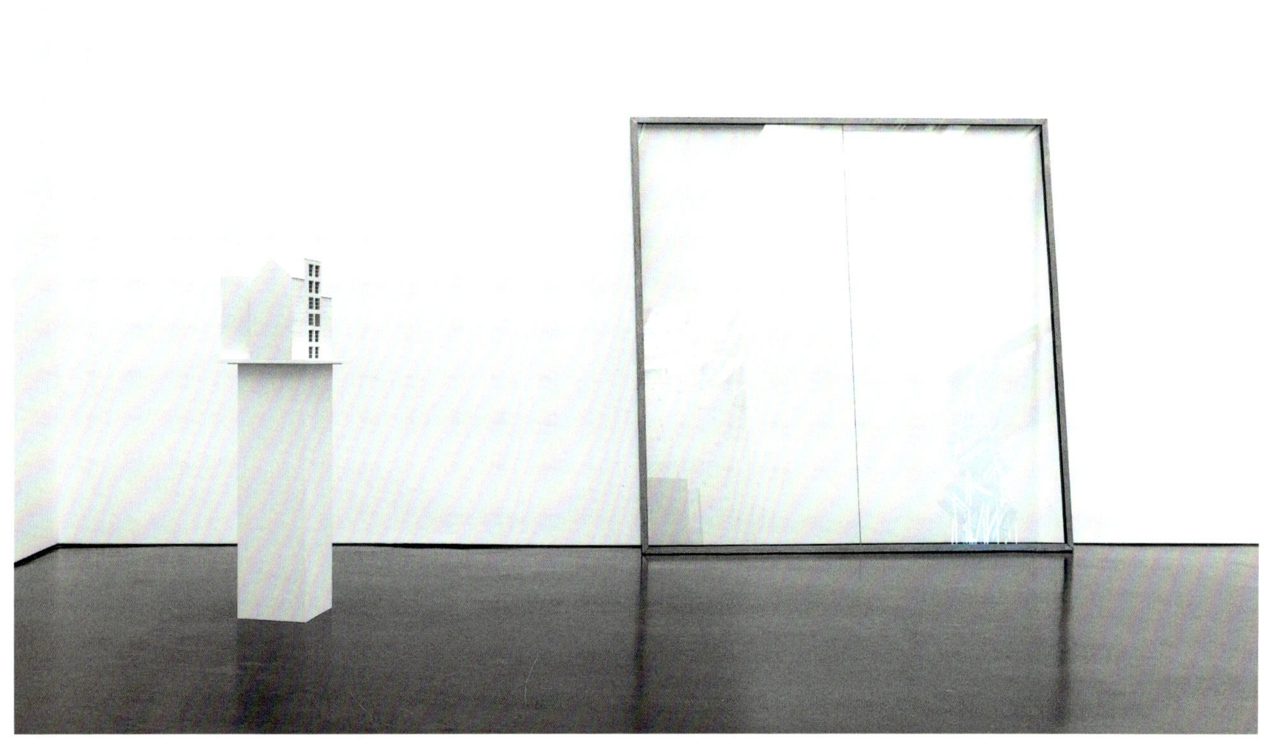

**Isa Genzken**
Fenster, Venloer Straße 21, 1988,
Model, 2015

Großes Fenster, 1987/88

# Rosemarie Trockel

# Rosemarie Trockel

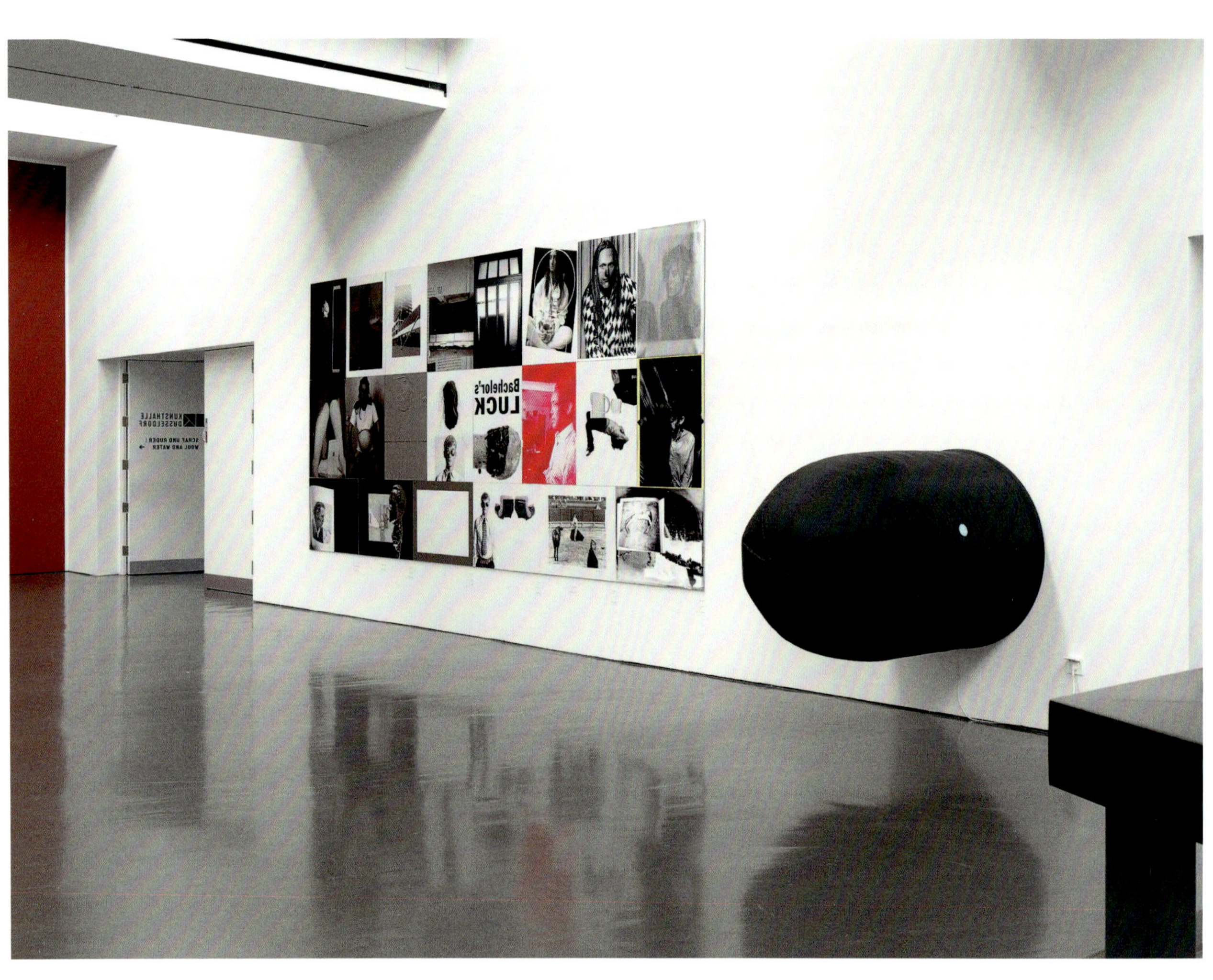
Bachelor's
LUCK

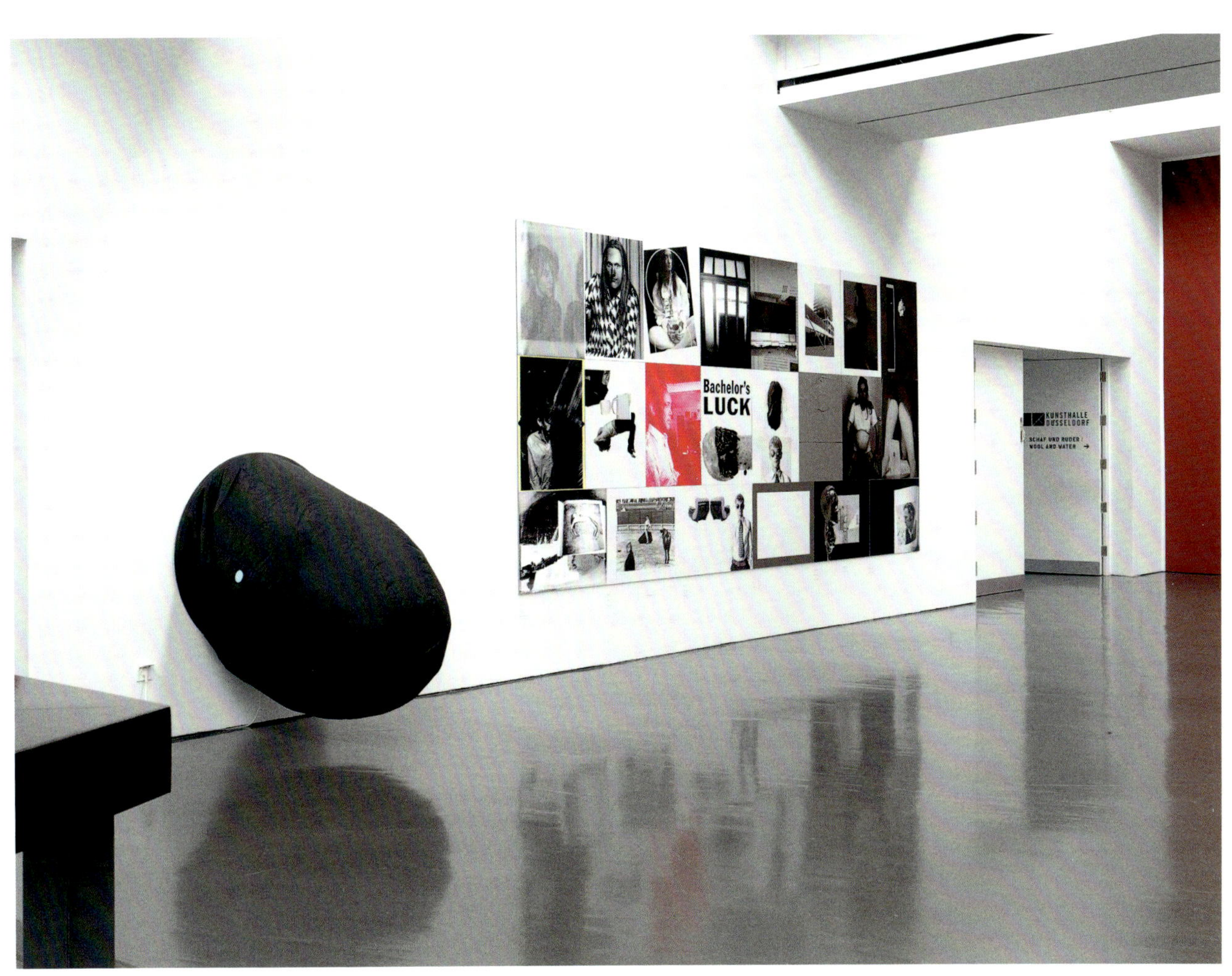


**Rosemarie Trockel**
My generation, no meat, 2000

CLUSTER I – Bachelor's Luck, 2015

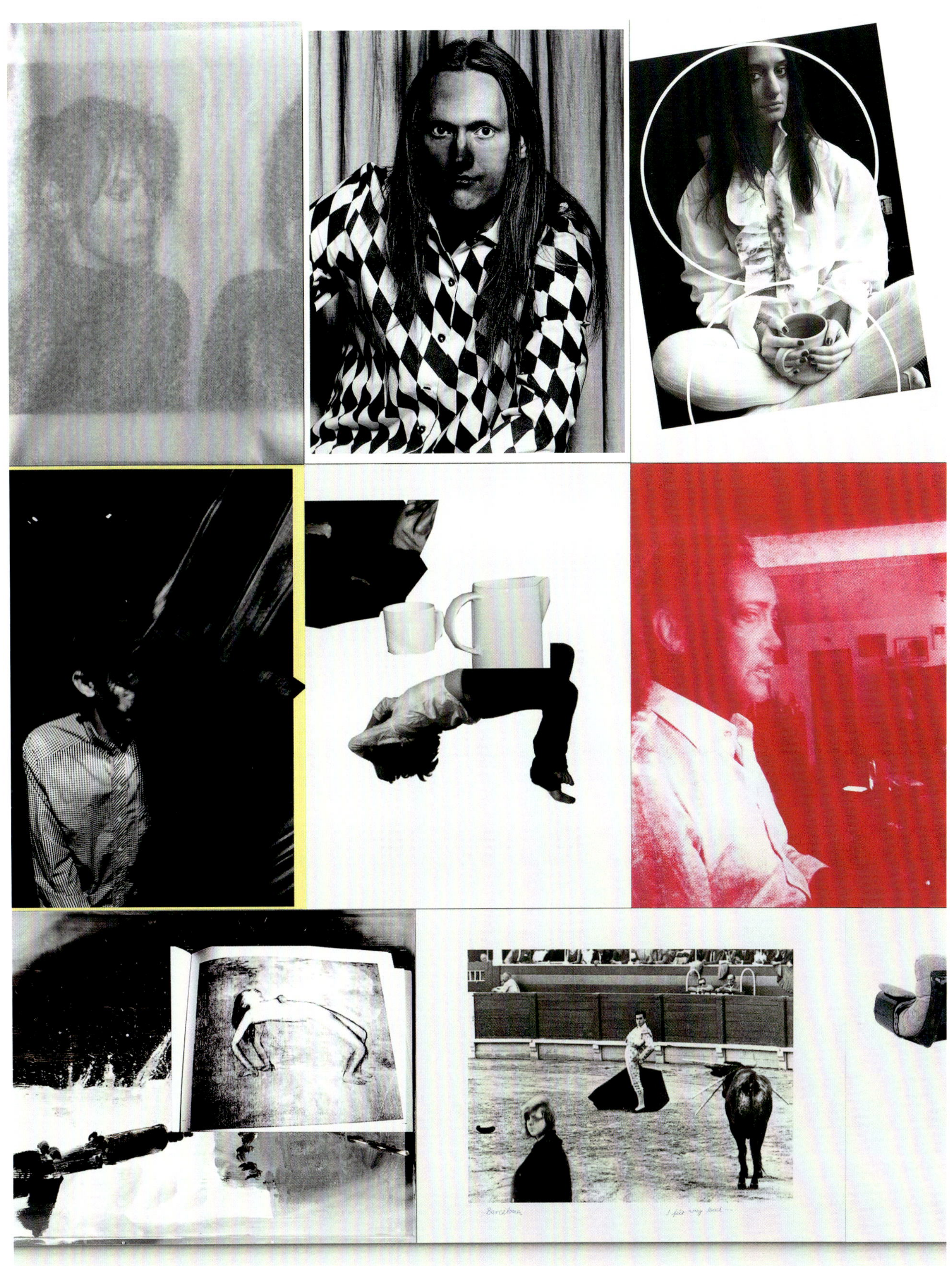

**Rosemarie Trockel**
CLUSTER I – Bachelor's Luck, 2015 (Detail)

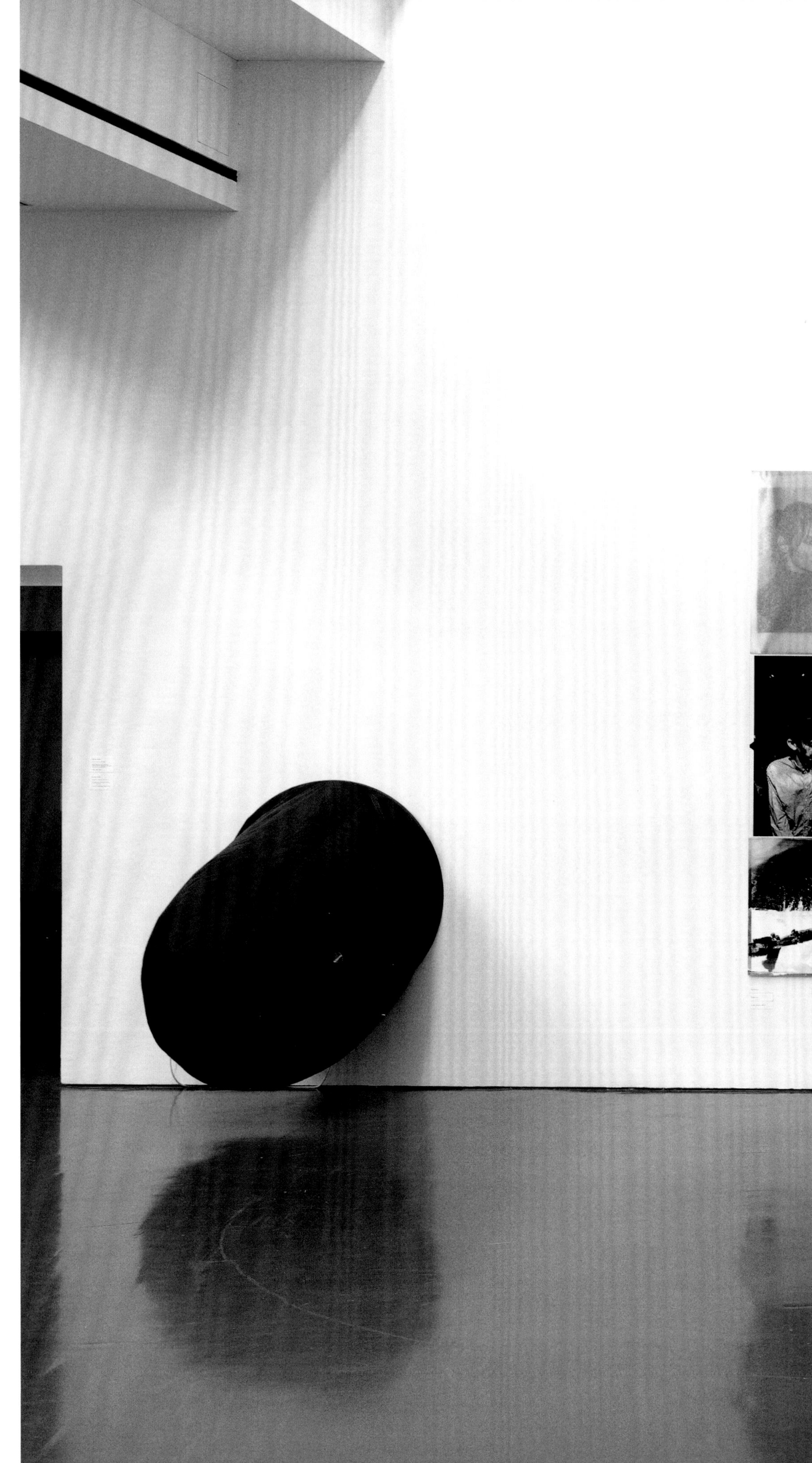

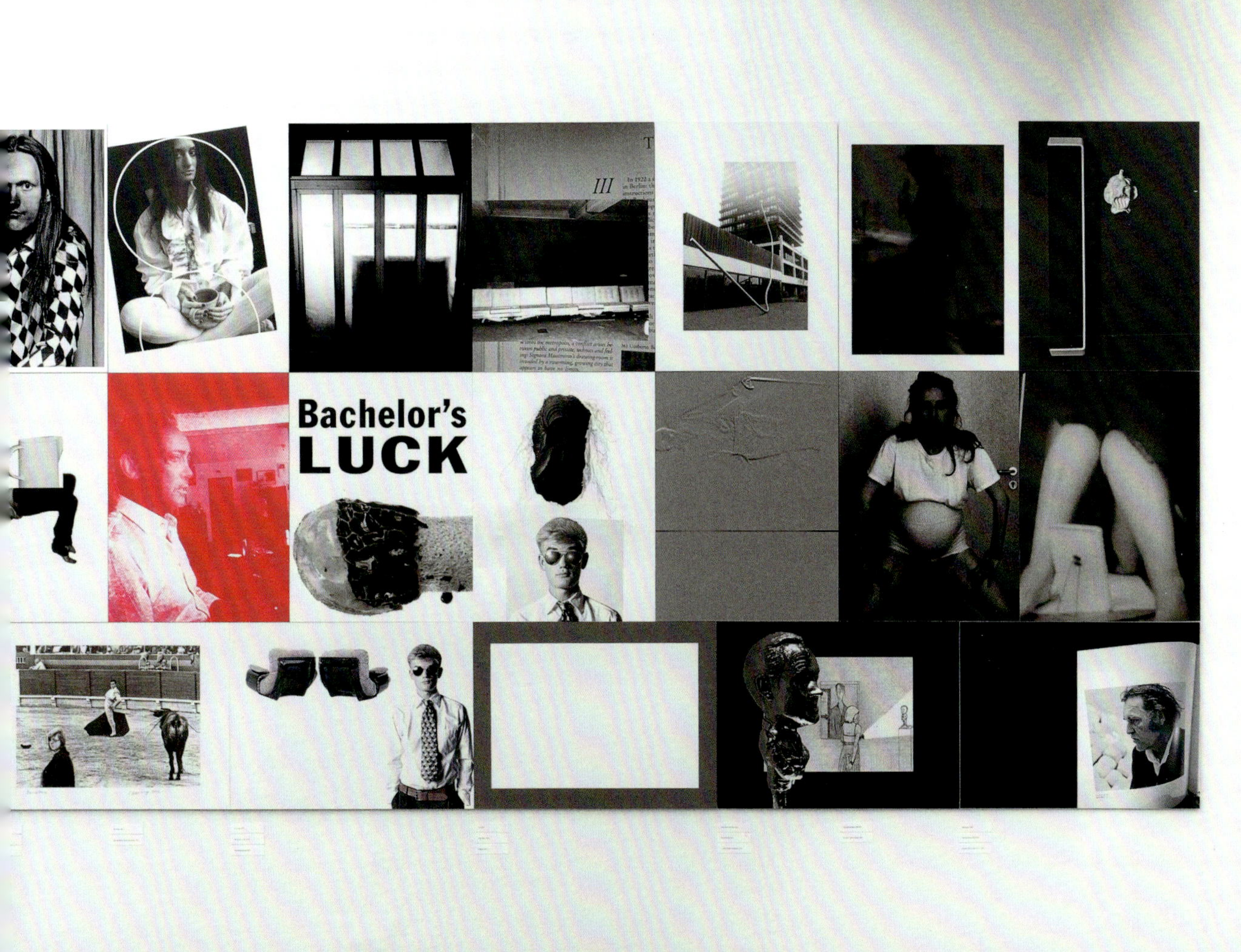
Bachelor's
LUCK

# Appendix

## WERKLISTE / LIST OF WORKS

### Lili Dujourie

(*1941 in Roeselare, Belgien / *Belgium*)
lebt und arbeitet in Lovendegem, Belgien / *lives and works in Lovendegem, Belgium*

**Untitled,** 1967
Stahl / *Steel*
Courtesy die Künstlerin / *The artist*

**Untitled,** 1967
Armierter Stahl / *Reinforced steel*
Courtesy die Künstlerin / *The artist*

**Untitled,** 1970
Stahl / *Steel*
Courtesy Galerie Micheline Szwajcer, Brüssel

**Amerikaans Imperialism,** 1972–2016
Wandfarbe und Stahl / *Wall paint and steel*
Courtesy die Künstlerin / *The artist*

**Effen Spiegel van een stille stroom,** 1976
Video, 13:43 min.
Courtesy die Künstlerin / *The artist*

**Portret,** 1985
Spiegel und Holz / *Mirror and wood*
Courtesy Galerie Micheline Szwajcer, Brüssel

**Between Black and Pink,** 1986
Spiegel, Eisen, Samttuch / *Mirror, iron, velvet fabric*
Belfius Art Collection

**Portret,** 1987
Granit und Spiegel / *Granite and mirror*
Courtesy die Künstlerin / *The artist*

### Isa Genzken

(*1948 in Bad Oldesloe, Schleswig-Holstein)
lebt und arbeitet / *lives and works* in Berlin

**Großes Fenster,** 1987/88
Stahl und Glas / *Steel and glass*
Courtesy Private Collection Alexander Schröder, Berlin

**Fenster, Venloer Straße 21,** 1988
Cologne, Galerie Daniel Buchholz
Realized / not installed

Model, 2015; scale 1:50
Plastik, Acrylfarbe, Metall, Acryl-Glas, Holz / *Plastic, acrylic paint, metal, acrylic glass, wood*
Courtesy Galerie Buchholz, Köln/Berlin

### Astrid Klein

(*1951 in Köln / *Cologne*)
lebt und arbeitet in Köln und Leipzig / *lives and works in Cologne and Leipzig*

**Ohne Titel (Sie interessiert der Raum?...),** 1979
Verschiedene Materialien auf Leinwand / *Mixed media on canvas*
Courtesy SCHAUWERK Sindelfingen

**Fly Catcher III,** 1987–91
Leuchtstoffröhre, Insektenfänger, Stahlrohr, Bewegungsmelder, Transformator / *Fluorescent lamps, insect catcher, steel pipe, motion detectors, transformers*

**Corriger la fortune (From the series of the white paintings),** 1988
Acryl, Quartz, Alabastergips, Zinkoxyd, Foto auf Leinwand / *Acrylic, quartz crystal, alabaster plaster, zinc white, photography on canvas*

**Untitled,** 1993/2011
Spiegel / *Mirror*

**Untitled (Wie kommt die Zeit ins Hirn, Centralnervös),** 1998
Neon, Seil, Kette / *Neon, rope, chain*

**Untitled (If you want something ... ),** 2012
Gießharz, Metall-Pigment, Karton, Band, Fotopapier / *Cast resin, pigment, cardboard, tape, photographic paper, metal coated (aluminium)*

**Untitled (Le spectacle n'arrête pas),** 2012
Gießharz, Pigment, Karton, Band, Text / *Cast resin, pigment, cardboard, tape, text*

Courtesy Sprüth Magers Berlin London

### Mischa Kuball

(*1959 in Düsseldorf)
lebt und arbeitet / *lives and works* in Düsseldorf

**‚platon's spiegel',** 2009
Videoprojektion, / *Video projection,* 21 min.
225 x 318 cm

**‚platon's spiegel' Dokumentation 1,** 2011
Video, 45 min.

**‚platon's spiegel'**
**Dokumentation 2,** 2011
Video, 45 min.

Courtesy der Künstler / *The artist*

**Aron Mehzion**

(*1970 in Asmara, Eritrea)
lebt und arbeitet / *lives and works* in Düsseldorf

**Passage VII,** 2016
Zeichnung auf eloxiertem Aluminium (Messing) / *Drawing on anodized aluminium (brass)*

**Passage VIII,** 2016
Zeichnung auf eloxiertem Aluminium (Messing) / *Drawing on anodized aluminium (brass)*

**A I A,** 2016
Semitransparentes Spiegelglas, Travertin, Messing, Objekte / *Semitransparent mirror glass, travertine, brass, objects*

**A' I A',** 2016
Semitransparentes Spiegelglas, Travertin, Messing, Objekte / *Semitransparent mirror glass, travertine, brass, objects*

Courtesy Daniel Marzona, Berlin

**A I A',** 2016
Semitransparentes Spiegelglas, Travertin, Messing, Objekte / *Semitransparent mirror glass, travertine, brass, objects*
Privatsammlung / *Private Collection*

**Non fatto con le mani,** 2016
Semitransparentes Spiegelglas, Travertin, Messing, Objekte / *Semitransparent mirror glass, travertine, brass, objects*
Egidio Marzona, Berlin

**Reinhard Mucha**

(*1950 in Düsseldorf)
lebt / *lives* in Düsseldorf

**Probestück, Studio Piece**, 1982

Massivholz *(2 Stühle, Fundstücke)*, Tischlerplatte *(Sockel)*
206,5 × 45,0 × 63,0 cm

Courtesy Privatsammlung

---

**Probestück, Studio Piece**, 1982

Solid wood *(two chairs)*, blockboard *(pedestal)*
81.30 × 17.72 × 24.80 inches

Courtesy Private Collection

© Mucha 2016

**O.T. – Oberer Totpunkt, T.D.C. – Top Dead Center**, [1989] 1985

Massivholz, Floatglas, Opalglas *(Ausstellungsvitrine)*, Vierkantstahlrohr verchromt, Hartholz, Stoff *(2 gepolsterte Bürostühle)*, Alkydharzlackfarbe, Tischlerplatte *(Sockel)*
266,5 × 101,5 × 96,5 cm

Courtesy Privatsammlung

---

**O.T. – Oberer Totpunkt, T.D.C. – Top Dead Center**, [1989] 1985

Solid wood, float glass, opal glass *(display case)*, chrome plated steel square tube, hardwood, fabric *(2 upholstered office chairs)*, alkyd enamel paint, blockboard *(pedestal)*
104.92 × 39.96 × 37.99 inches

Courtesy Private Collection

© Mucha 2016

**Oderin / Ohne Titel** (MÄNNER FRAUEN), [1987] 1987 / 1981

**Oderin**
Filz, Tischlerplatte *(2 Sockel)*, PVC, Metall *(4 Fußbänke)*, Massivholz *(Fußbank, Fundstück)*
181,5 × 225 × 383 cm
**Ohne Titel** (MÄNNER FRAUEN)
Alkydharzlackfarbe, Metall, Floatglas, Alkydharzlackfarbe rückseitig auf Glas gemalt, Filz, Holz, Leuchtstofflampe, Elektrokabel, Winkelstecker mit Kippschalter, 2 Kabelbinder, Klebeband, Verlängerungskabel mit Kupplung und Stecker
140 × 385 × 12,5 cm (MÄNNER)
215 × 465 × 18 cm inklusive Lampe + Anschluß (FRAUEN)

Installationsmaße Kunsthalle Düsseldorf 215 × 400 × 530 cm

Courtesy Privatsammlung Stuttgart

---

**Oderin / Untitled** (MÄNNER FRAUEN), [1987] 1987 / 1981
Two-part work ensemble

**Oderin**
Felt, blockboard *(2 pedestals)*, PVC, metal *(4 footstools)*, solid wood *(foodstool, found object)*
71.46 × 88.58 × 150.79 inches
**Untitled** (MÄNNER FRAUEN)
Alkyd enamel paint, metal, float glass, alkyd enamel painted on reverse of glass, felt, wood, fluorescent lamp, electrical cord, angle plug with rocker switch, 2 zip ties, adhesive tape, extension cord with male plug and female plug
55.12 × 151.57 × 4.92 inches (MÄNNER)
84.65 × 183.07 × 7.09 inches including lamp + plug (FRAUEN)

Installation dimensions Kunsthalle Düsseldorf 84.65 × 157.48 × 208.66 inches

Courtesy Private Collection Stuttgart

© Mucha 2016

**Zwei Photos ohne Titel** [*Ohne Titel (Oberhausen)*], [2003] 1983
Auflage: 25 Exemplare

Massivholz profiliert und altsilber patiniert *(Rahmen)*, UV-Schutzglas, säurefreier Museumskarton, 2 Silbergelatine Prints auf Barytpapier
41,8 × 72,7 × 2,7 cm

Courtesy Privatsammlung

---

**Two untitled photographs** [*Untitled (Oberhausen)*], [2003] 1983
Edition: 25 copies

Wooden picture mouldings with coin finish *(frame)*, UV protection glass, acid free museum board, 2 silver gelatine prints on baryta paper
16.46 × 28.62 × 1.06 inches

Courtesy Private Collection

© Mucha 2016

**Vier Photos ohne Titel** [*Ohne Titel (Oberhausen) / Urlaub im All*], [2003] 1983/1988

Massivholz profiliert und altsilber patiniert *(Rahmen)*, UV-Schutzglas, säurefreier Museumskarton, 4 Silbergelatine Prints auf Barytpapier
57,5 × 72,4 × 2,7 cm

Courtesy der Künstler und Sprüth Magers

---

**Four untitled photographs** [*Untitled (Oberhausen) / Holiday in Space*], [2003] 1983/1988

Wooden picture mouldings with coin finish *(frame)*, UV protection glass, acid free museum board, 4 silver gelatine prints on baryta paper
22.64 × 28.50 × 1.06 inches

Courtesy the artist and Sprüth Magers

© Mucha 2016

**Edition 1991 – >>Kreuzstück<<**, 2004
Diptychon
Auflage: 25 Unikate + 3 a. p.

Linker Tondo
Glashalter, 2 Floatglasscheiben, Alkydharzlackfarbe rückseitig auf Glas gemalt, *Buchseite* Offset beidseitig *(Fundstück)*, Filz
ø 38 cm × 4,6 cm
Rechter Tondo
Glashalter, Floatglasscheibe, Aluminiumscheibe
ø 34 cm × 4,6 cm

*Jedes Exemplar mit unterschiedlicher Hinterglasbemalung.*
*Zugehöriger Aufbewahrungskasten mit beschriftetem Schiebedeckel*
Alkydharzlackfarbe, Holz, *ein vom Künstler gestaltetes, nummeriertes und signiertes Deckblatt als Zertifikat mit 4 reproduzierten Photographien des Künstlers*
Offset *45,5 × 45,5 cm, paßgenaue Innenauspolsterung 17,6 × 49 × 49 cm*

Courtesy der Künstler und Galerie Bärbel Grässlin

---

**Edition 1991 – >>Kreuzstück<<**, 2004
Diptych
Edition: 25 unique pieces + 3 a. p.

Left tondo
Metal shoulder clamps, 2 float glass discs, alkyd enamel painted on reverse of glass, *book page* offset print double-sided *(found object)*, felt
ø 14.96 inches × 1.81 inches
Right tondo
Metal shoulder clamps, float glass disc, aluminum disc
ø 13.39 inches × 1.81 inches

*Each piece painted differently on reverse of glass.*
*With custom fabricated storage crate, signage on the sliding cover*
enamel paint, wood *including a cover sheet as certificate designed, numbered and signed by the artist with 4 reproduced photographs from the artist*
offset *17.91 x 17.91 inches, special made inner cushion 6.93 x 19.29 x 19.29 inches*

Courtesy the artist and Galerie Bärbel Grässlin

© Mucha 2016

**Werden**, 2016

Glashalter, Floatglas, Alkydharzlackfarbe rückseitig auf Glas gemalt, Aluminiumprofile, *Zinkblechwanne* verzinktes Stahlblech, Massivholz *(Fundstück)*, Glasspiegel, Multiplex-Sperrholz
78,6 × 126 × 23,8 cm

Courtesy Sprüth Magers

---

**Werden**, 2016

Metal shoulder clamps, float glass, alkyd enamel painted on reverse of glass, aluminum profiles, *zinc tub* zinc-coated steel sheet, solid wood *(found object)*, glass mirror, multilayer-plywood
30.94 × 49.61 × 9.37 inches

Courtesy Sprüth Magers

© Mucha 2016

**Gerhard Richter**

(*1932 in Dresden)
lebt und arbeitet in Köln / *lives and works in Cologne*

**Spiegel,** 1981
Kunsthalle Düsseldorf

**Sturtevant**

(*1930 in Lakewood, Ohio †2014 in Paris)

**Duchamp – Man Ray Portrait,** 1966
Fotografie (schwarz-weiß) / *Photography (b/w)*

**Duchamp – Relâche,** 1967
Fotografie (schwarz-weiß) / *Photography (b/w)*

**Duchamp – Nu descendant un escalier,** 1968
Film-Still / *Film still*

**Scale Model for Gober Wall Paper,** 1994
Kreide und Collage auf Tafel / *Chalk and collage on black board*

**Study for Gober Dick Paper,** 1994
Kreide auf Tafel / *Chalk on black board*

Courtesy Galerie Hans Mayer, Düsseldorf

**Rosemarie Trockel**

(*1952 in Schwerte, Nordrhein-Westfalen)
lebt und arbeitet in Köln / *lives and works in Cologne*

**My generation, no meat,** 2000
Mixed Media (Holz, Stoff, Elektromotor, Ventilator, Knöpfe) / *Mixed media (wood, fabric, electric motor, ventilator, buttons)*
Courtesy Sprüth Magers

**CLUSTER I – Bachelor's Luck,** 2015
22 Digitalprints auf Alu-Dibond / *22 digital prints on alu-dibond*
Courtesy Privatsammlung / *Private collection*

Conte Nikos Araldi di Piadena, Jochen Arentzen, Ralf Berger, Bénédicte Bouton, Daniel Buchholz, Wilfried & Yannicke Cooreman, Carla Donauer, Katharina Forero, Claudia Friedrich, Miriam Geisler, Martin Germann, Bärbel Grässlin, Thomas Grässlin & Nanette Hagstotz, David Gray, Wolfgang Günzel, Alexander Hattwig, Berit Homburg, Hans- Joachim Hüsgen, Sigrid & Klaus Konopka, Achim Kukulies, Doris Krystof, Simone Kunz, Ludmilla Lencsés, Karsten Löckemann, Philomene Magers, Daniel Marzona, Egidio Marzona, Hans Mayer, Marie Mayer, Rita McBride, Monika Mucha, Werner Raeune, Friedrich E. Rentschler & Maria Schlumberger-Rentschler, Thomas W. Rieger, Rolf Sachs, Schauwerk Sindelfingen, Andreas Schleicher-Lange, Rüdiger Schöttle, Volker Schräger-Enkirch, Alexander Schröder, Kim Sluijter, Monika Sprüth, Micheline Szwajcer, Susanne Titz, Franco Ubbriaco, Hilde Vanfleteren, Jan Wagner, Thomas Wong und weiteren privaten Leihgebern, die ungenannt bleiben wollen / *et al., along with private lenders who wish to remain unnamed.*

Für die erfolgreiche Durchführung der Ausstellung und des Katalogs möchte ich vor allem den KünstlerInnen Lili Dujourie, Isa Genzken, Astrid Klein, Mischa Kuball, Aron Mehzion, Reinhard Mucha, Rosemarie Trockel und Gerhard Richter meinen Dank aussprechen. Ihrer großzügigen Unterstützung und Ermutigung gilt meine tiefe Dankbarkeit. / *I am indebted to many people for their support and encouragement which was invaluable for the successful completion of both the exhibition and the catalogue, especially to the artists Lili Dujourie, Isa Genzken, Astrid Klein, Mischa Kuball, Aron Mehzion, Reinhard Mucha, Rosemarie Trockel, and Gerhard Richter.*

Zu guter Letzt möchte ich mich bei meinem gesamten Team der Kunsthalle Düsseldorf, bei Christan Boros und Uta Grosenick vom DISTANZ Verlag und bei Lisa Pommerenke für die Gestaltung des Katalogs bedanken. / *Last but by no means least, I would like to thank my whole awesome team at Kunsthalle Düsseldorf, Christan Boros and Uta Grosenick from DISTANZ Verlag, and Lisa Pommerenke for the graphic design. Thank you all.*

## IMPRESSUM / IMPRINT


Dieser Katalog erscheint anlässlich der Ausstellung / *This catalogue is published on the occasion of the exhibition*

**Schaf und Ruder / Wool and Water**
Kunsthalle Düsseldorf
1. Oktober – 27. November 2016
*October 1 – November 27, 2016*

**Kurator / *Curator***
Gregor Jansen

**Verwaltung / *Administration***
Lumnije Sturr

**Leitung Ausstellungstechnik / *Head of the Installation Staff***
Jörg Schlürscheid

**Haustechnik / *Building Services***
Arno Götzen

**Ausstellung / Exhibition**

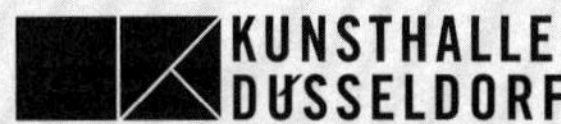


Kunsthalle Düsseldorf gGmbH
Grabbeplatz 4
40213 Düsseldorf
Tel. +49 (0)211 89 96 243
Fax +49 (0)211 89 29 168
mail@kunsthalle-duesseldorf.de
www.kunsthalle-duesseldorf.de

**Direktor / *Director***
Gregor Jansen

**Kaufmännische Geschäftsführerin / *Managing Director***
Ariane Berger

**Kuratorinnen / *Curators***
Anna Brohm, Jasmina Merz, Anna Lena Seiser

**Wissenschaftliches Volontariat / *Assistant Curator***
Dana Bergmann

**Presse und Kommunikation, Kunstvermittlung / *Press and Communication, Education***
Dirk Schewe

**Direktionsassistenz und Kunstvermittlung / *Assistant to the Director and Education***
Claudia Paulus

**Mit freundlicher Unterstützung von / *With kind support of***

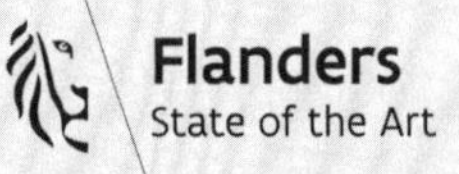


**Die Kunsthalle Düsseldorf wird gefördert durch / *Kunsthalle Düsseldorf is funded by***

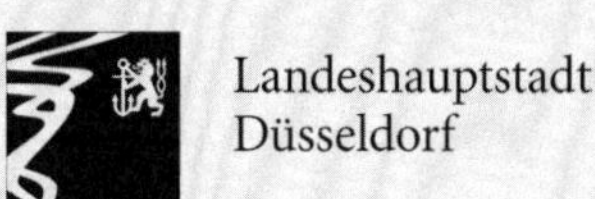


**Ständige Partner der Kunsthalle Düsseldorf / *Permanent Partners of Kunsthalle Düsseldorf***

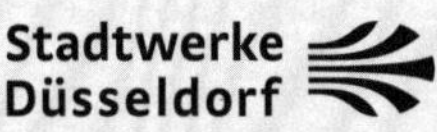


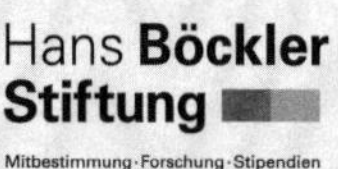

**Katalog / Catalogue**

**Herausgeber / *Editor***
Gregor Jansen, Kunsthalle Düsseldorf

**Grafik / *Graphic Design***
Lisa Pommerenke

**Autor / *Author***
Gregor Jansen

**Redaktionelle Mitarbeit / *Editorial Assistants***
Dana Bergmann, Anna Lena Seiser

**Lektorat / *Copy Editing***
Kirsten Rachowiak, München

**Übersetzung / *Translation***
Anthony DePasquale

**Bildbearbeitung / *Lithography***
Joseph Sappler

**Produktion / *Production Management***
DISTANZ Verlag, Sonja Bahr

**Gesamtherstellung / *Production***
DZA Druckerei zu Altenburg GmbH



**Vertrieb / *Distribution***
Gestalten, Berlin
www.gestalten.com
sales@gestalten.com

ISBN 978-3-95476-179-1
Printed in Germany

**Erschienen im / *Published by***
DISTANZ Verlag
www.distanz.de

**BILDNACHWEISE / PHOTO CREDITS**